# EGG ON MY FACE

Seán Power
editor

GILL & MACMILLAN

Gill & Macmillan Ltd
Goldenbridge
Dublin 8
with associated companies throughout the world
© Introduction and selection Seán Power 1996
0 7171 2541 6


Design and print origination by
*Deirdre's Desktop*
Printed by
ColourBooks Ltd, Dublin

A catalogue record is available for this book from the British
Library.

1   3   5   4   2

# Contents

# INTRODUCTION

Shortly after *Those were the Days* was published, to raise funds for the Cancer Unit of the Children's Hospital in Crumlin, a group of us was gathered at a friend's house in Newbridge, Co. Kildare.

The reviews were great and Gill & Macmillan were confident that the first edition of the book — a compilation of Irish childhood memories from famous Irish people — would be sold out within a few months, a prediction that thankfully proved correct.

'I've got egg all over my face, Seán,' one of the lads confessed. 'I never thought I'd see the day when one of my friends would have a bestseller on his hands.'

'"Egg on My Face" — what a great name for a book,' another member of the group suggested. 'You should get all those famous personalities who gave you their childhood memories, to tell you their most embarrassing moments as well. That would give you the makings of another great book for the Crumlin Cancer Fund.'

'No, you'd never get famous people to write down their embarrassing moments for everybody to read,' somebody else said. 'Embarrassing moments are something you want to forget, not to recall for the whole nation to laugh at.'

The debate raged on, and by the end of the night I was determined to try the idea out and to see what the response would be.

More in hope than anything else, I sent out the first batch of letters in February 1996, asking those personalities who had contributed to *Those were the Days*, to take up their pens once more and to reveal an embarrassing moment or two from their past.

The replies began to roll in. Some of the original contributors were unable to come up with an appropriate 'embarrassing' moment but wished us well, and we decided to widen the net and invite new writers on board.

The response was wonderful and as the 'embarrassing moments' began to arrive they created their own moments at home. During my lunch, one day, I started to read one of the stories; to the surprise of my sons, I burst out laughing, spraying crumbs all over the table. Robert asked, 'Daddy, what's so funny?' I replied, 'Ah, it's a story from Paddy Murray, you can read it later.'

As you will soon see, some of the stories are real classics, like Jonathan Irwin's encounter with Sharon Stone, Hugh Leonard's faux pas with Sophia Loren, and Mike Burns' late-night visit to the wrong hotel bedroom.

The range and variety of the stories recalled is huge — grave-digging in a County Clare cemetery with the legendary Ned Cash; carrying out high-speed repairs with a fishing line on a nun's dishevelled habit by Sister Consilio; raiding the orchard of All Hallows College by Bertie Ahern and a young hit-squad.

Mary Harney reveals for the first time what it was she dropped that Bill Clinton picked up for her, in front of the TV cameras of the world, when the President of the USA visited Ireland; and Paddy Cullen recalls his dreadful memory from the 1978 All-Ireland when Mikey Sheehy chipped the ball over his head into the Dublin net, with Paddy believing all the time that referee Seamus Aldridge had given the free to Dublin instead of Kerry.

Father Brian D'Arcy recalls the day he got drunk saying Mass in Lourdes; *Sunday Independent* editor, Aengus Fanning, regales us with his efforts to provide the best 'May Altar' in his primary school; and Heinz boss, Tony O'Reilly, remembers his final game for the Irish rugby team in 1970, when he was knocked unconscious and some of the Irish supporters wanted to knock his chauffeur unconscious too. No less than three bishops have contributed their memories also.

I am particularly delighted to have contributions from a number of County Kildare based writers, including Des Egan, John MacKenna, Des Maguire, Monica Carr, Chris

Glennon, Eoghan Corry, Stan Cosgrove, Larry Tompkins and Dermot Earley, as well as from Kildare politicians like Charlie McCreevy, Timmy Conway and my own father, Paddy.

To all the contributors to the book, many, many thanks. You have saved me from what could have been a very embarrassing moment.

I must thank Des Maguire, Breda Gleeson and John Treacy for their continuing invaluable advice and help. Many thanks to Sinead McSweeney, whose work and support is very much appreciated.

To my secretary, Margaret, who worked so hard in making the book possible, I am deeply indebted.

To my wife, Deirdre, and family, I extend a very special thanks for all their help, encouragement and patience. These are the people who have had to share, enjoy, witness, cringe, cry and laugh at many of *my* embarrassing moments.


Seán Power
August 1996

# Bertie Ahern

There is one moment locked in time like a freeze frame on the video recorder which still brings flashes of red to my cheeks when I remember the sounds, the looks, the shame and the flood of red tide which covered my face. I was 9 or 10 at the time, beginning to be aware of a bigger world out there, moving to the skiffle beat, Man. United, the Olympics, and beginning to understand a little about the political shape of Ireland. My world was Drumcondra, and while we ranged as far afield as Fairview Park, Santry Woods and the Stadium, the Phoenix Park and the Hill of Howth, by and large most of our play and activities took place in Drumcondra. And the centre of that world was Church Avenue where we lived, and All Hallows, where my dad was farm manager, and an extremely hard-working one at that, for all of my youth.

It had been an extraordinary fine summer which we had spent entirely out of doors, with plenty of bus rides out to Dollyer and once out to Sutton with Mick whose uncle had a big house out there on the beach. As we returned to school in September we exchanged tales of derring-do during the holiers and spoke of hardly anything else but the upcoming All Ireland Hurling and Football finals. And one other topical issue: orchards!

There was nothing on earth to compare with the thrill of robbing an orchard, being chased by a mad dog and enjoying the sweet juicy taste of the stolen fruit. There was a special taste, a special crunch when your top teeth closed down on the mottled-red taut surface and came away with a half-moon of pilfered pleasure.

That year the best of the apples were in All Hallows. That presented me with two different dilemmas: one, how to conjure up that spirit of forbidden fruit, when my father could slip me one from time to time; and secondly, how to launch a proper raid under the eagle-eyed protection of my ever vigilant dad.

Both dilemmas were resolved by powerful external forces. An edict issues from the President's office — no, not the one in the Park, but the real President of All Hallows — that no one was to even dream of touching, much less plucking, the rosy-red lovelies of the inner garden. That edict in itself was sufficient reason to warrant an immediate offensive on the citadel! And as luck would have it, a gathering of Old IRA veterans near the GPO the following Sunday meant that, for once, my father would be absent for a few precious hours.

Our plan was executed with military precision. Our six-man crew posted three nixers on the look-out at each of the three main gates, and our youngest member, Sean, hid behind a bush beside the path leading up to the college. We bagged forty-five of the rosiest, reddest, most gorgeous Garden of Eden apples, which could well explain how easily Eve fell. We were in and out of there in twenty minutes flat. And I had my share secreted under a pile of dock leaves in the back garden, to be taken to school next day, all except the one I had stuffed into my trousers pocket.

Dad had barely returned and begun to give a blow-by-blow account of a heated republican afternoon by the pillars of our independence, when there was a loud banging on the door. With a face redder than any Beauty of Bath, there stood the college president in a fit of apocalyptic apoplexy.

'They're gone, Con, they're gone. Every last one of them. Robbed and raided under our very eyes. Do you know anyone in the guards, or who do you think would do such a thing at all, at all?'

My father brought him into the sitting-room (we called it the front room) used only for state occasions and visiting dignitaries. Tea and cake were ferried in twice, and then with a brief glance into the kitchen and a sharp 'God bless' he was gone. It was almost bedtime. My father was listening to 'Question Time' with Joe Linnane, and my mother was ironing our school shirts with the old solid iron.

I sniffled once. 'Would you ever use your handkerchief and blow your nose, and not be sniffling', said my mam sideways, without turning around. Without thinking, I reached deep into my pocket and pulled out the hanky. For a moment the rosy-red secret seemed to be suspended by extraterrestrial forces in mid-air, defying all the laws of natural gravity. Then it bumped loudly on the lino, rolled two feet and stopped against my father's hobnailed boots. My heart stopped. The contestant on the radio who had been asked the capital of outer Mongolia stopped. My mother stopped. The world stopped. And my father was looking at me with narrowed, understanding eyes. A red tide of shame and embarrassment filled my every nerve end, every blood vessel and capillary of my face. It was my most embarrassing moment.

I shall draw the cloak of personal dignity and years around the sequel. Put it this way: there was no way I was ever going to be invited to join the president for high tea. I couldn't have sat down anyway, even if I had.

# CHARLIE BIRD

Most people forget a name from time to time. Indeed, when it comes to remembering names I'm not the best in the world. But to do so on television in the middle of a live news bulletin is neither clever nor something which enhances one's career. When I think of some of my most embarrassing moments, I break out in a cold sweat.

Which of the many should I relate? The time the Labour leader, Dick Spring, kicked me on the shin to stop the interview I was conducting with him. This happened during the life of the Coalition headed up by Dr Garret FitzGerald. Dick Spring recalls the story somewhat differently to me. We laugh about it now and as he says himself, it was only a tap, 'an ankle tap'. But it was certainly one way to end a television interview.

I mustn't digress; back to my story. Every time I see Trevor Sargent, the TD for the Green Party in Dublin, I remember that Sunday evening at the Ballsbridge count centre for the European elections in June 1989.

I was scheduled to do a live insert into the Nine o'clock News on the latest state of the count. The afternoon and evening had not been particularly busy. I had my clipboard and the main points of the story well prepared, in other words well rehearsed: often a fatal mistake. As usual at these events the people at the count centre tend to gravitate towards where the television camera is placed.

Nine o'clock came and all eyes inside the count centre were focused on Mr Bird who was about to pronounce on the possible outcome of the election in the Dublin area. The red light on the outside broadcast camera went on, and I heard the newscaster in the studio at Donnybrook hand over to Charlie Bird for the results in the European elections in Dublin.

If you can excuse the pun, I got off to a flying start, until I came to the section of my report which dealt with the vote of the Green Party candidate . . . Alas, a couple of minutes earlier I could reel off the names of all the candidates, but in that instant, gone into cyberspace or somewhere else was the name of the Green Party candidate. I looked at the camera. I looked at the red light and time seemed to stand still. The crowd around me were hushed, listening to my every word. But, alas, nothing happened . . . Total blank. Seconds passed . . . Life seemed to pass me by. Every broadcaster's nightmare. A stillness. I even had time to notice a beam of sunshine streaming down into the hall. There I was, alone in the world, yet in front of the whole country.

Then I heard the prompt from the floor manager, 'Sargent. His name is Sargent.' Suddenly the cold sweat turned to a swimming sensation, and with one mighty leap the name Trevor Sargent blurted out. I finished my report like a true professional, my pride hurt and my nerves ajangle.

Afterwards, the floor manager, a well-known character in RTE by the name of Tadgh De Brun, turned to me and said, 'That was a close one, Charlie. I knew that Green candidate had a name something to do with a policeman.'

I wasn't the first and won't be the last broadcaster to be dug out of a hole by an RTE floor manager.

If only it had been radio, I could have done what a famous colleague of mine did on one occasion. It was during the course of a general election count. John Bowman called the said individual in to give a breakdown of where the transfers were going in a particular constituency. Rather than face the embarrassment of having to admit he hadn't a clue where the transfers were going, he took off his headphones, put down his microphone and tiptoed out of the room.

As John Bowman was saying on air, 'We seem to be having difficulty getting back to that count . . .', a creaking sound, followed by a banging door could be heard. Alas, on that Sunday night at the RDS count centre, I had no such way of saving my embarrassment. However, I like the idea.

Perhaps what I should have done was to say to the people at home, 'Sorry, folks, I've forgotten that person's name', and then shouted to the crowd in the hall, 'Hi, what's the name of the Green Party candidate?'

# FATHER HARRY BOHAN

*'Hurling interest at fever pitch'*
*'Rousing welcome for Hurling Heroes'*
*'Proud to be a Clare man'*

These are a few headlines from the late 1970s, not from 1995. Hurling was indeed at fever pitch in County Clare and this team was capturing the imagination of people all over the country. Winning the first National League title in 1977 was a huge breakthrough after twenty-one years without any title. Retaining the title in 1978 and consistently meeting and beating the best ensured that Clare's hurling heroes of that period 'were showered with praise by all followers of the game and messages of congratulations poured in' (*Clare Champion*, 6 May 1977).

That gives you some idea of what was then regarded as a golden era in Clare hurling and a period which sowed the seeds for the heights the county has now scaled. Anthony Daly, the county's All-Ireland winning captain of 1995 has no doubt that his inspiration came from that team and period. His heroes were Sean Stack, John Callinan, Sean Hehir, Jackie O'Gorman, Ger Loughnane, Mick Moroney, Enda O'Connor, Noel Casey and Co. — all members of that team.

Why then do I turn to this period and this team for one of my most difficult moments? Embarrassing too, but it is not the word which really captures the mood of this particular happening.

Well, I was very proud to be manager of that team. We were playing Cork in the Munster final of 1977, a Cork team which had won three All-Irelands in a row and regarded as one of the best ever. We were playing very well, led them by 5 or 6 points and well capable of beating them and going on to win the All-Ireland. Shortly before half-time, our full back was sent off for something which to this day he and I are convinced he never did. Con Houlihan, writing in the *Evening Press* the following Wednesday, had this to say: 'The sending to the line of Jim Power was the main source of controversy last Sunday; if the people of Clare are bitter about it, we do not blame them.' The rest is history. We lost the final. If we had won it, who knows? Many would say that that team could have gone on to win a few All-Irelands.

Where is the embarrassment in all this? I suppose it is in the fact that against all the advice of shrewd GAA administrators, I called for an inquiry into the standard of refereeing in that final. The then Chairman of the County Board said we hadn't a snowball's chance in hell of getting a hearing from the Munster Council. That was how one newspaper put it. But the same paper went on, at length, to point out that the inquiry should be held. It became an embarrassment in that our request was not just turned down but dismissed out of hand. The Chairman of the Board was right. Whilst many believed it should have been held and it was justified, they also agreed that if it was held, it would have been totally unprecedented and the whole affair could have become a major embarrassment for the authorities.

It was never held, but its dismissal as an absurd suggestion became an embarrassment for me. I still sometimes wonder about it all.

# GILLIAN BOWLER

My most embarrassing moment? Quite frankly, it's hard to know where to begin, particularly as the really excruciating moments I wouldn't dream of sharing with anyone (unless after a bottle of wine, which the editor of this book hasn't stretched to yet).

I could start with the fact that this piece is only being written after a long moan and the knowledge that I promised it three weeks ago. But that doesn't really count as that's just guilt — never to be confused with the real culprit, embarrassment, which makes your stomach heave and your face flush with mortification months, even years, after the dreaded event.

I'm still embarrassed at the recollection of how, when locking myself out of my house, I called into a friendly neighbour to use the phone and organise spare keys. He, kind man, insisted I stay until the keys arrived and we got to chatting, in a desultory fashion, about the number of houses being built in our mews lane. We were happily agreeing that this was a good thing generally, price values going up, blah blah, when, desperately trying to prolong the conversation further, I commented, 'Apart from those four new houses they've just built near you' and, warming to my theme, 'Let's face it, for the money they must have spent, any self-respecting architect with a bit of imagination could have put up something halfway decent, instead of a dump that looks like an annexe of Mountjoy.'

You know the end to this story, don't you? And if I had the space there are so many more. Big mouth, big foot — that's me.

P.S. Mr Architect, I'm very sorry, and I've grown to love your houses.

# VINCENT BROWNE

It wasn't just because it was Louis Armstrong, it was because the celebrity was there (sorry, I'm going to name drop); yes, it was he, John Bowman, the earnest one with the ties and the fountain pen. The incident occurred in the Adelphi Cinema, Dublin, in July 1968.

I was working with RTE at the time on quite the worst programme that even it ever broadcast. It was called 'Roundabout Now'. Also working on it was Oliver Donoghue, now with the Irish Congress of Trade Unions, and two other people who have been lost in anonymity since then. One was a chap called Mike Bogdanov, who later had to make do with becoming director of the National Theatre in London, and a fellow called Terry Wogan. He was a quite promising fellow — no idea of what became of him!

I was a researcher cum interviewer on the programme. The previous week I had been in the programme office when a producer, Charlie Stuart, told me to be ready to travel to a stud farm in County Meath in a few minutes to interview Sir Gordon Richards. He gleaned from my reaction that I had never heard of Sir Gordon and muttered something about a repetition of the disaster of the previous week. I was advised to get briefed by Michael O'Hehir, whom I regarded as a demigod and hadn't dared approach previously in the television station. Michael O'Hehir was mystified how anybody who had never heard of Sir Gordon could be allowed in the door of RTE.

The interview with Sir Gordon took place in a field. The camera was behind my left shoulder and to my right, out of shot, I could see Charlie Stuart shake his head in disbelief with every inane question I put to the great man. When I asked a question that implied I understood there to be jumps in the Derby, Charlie buried his head in his hands — it was very off-putting for a serious interviewer.

For the following programme I was given a full week's preparation time. I was to do an interview with Louis Armstrong. I knew almost nothing about jazz, but I bought several books on the subject and having read these through I knew even less. In desperation I sought help and was advised to consult with Frank Hall who, I was told, knew everything about jazz. Frank agreed to assist and, very obligingly, offered to write out a series of questions — all I would have to do was to put these questions in sequence to Mr Armstrong. I didn't have to understand the questions.

The interview took place in a small dressing room in the Adelphi Cinema between two performances that Mr Armstrong was giving in the cinema that evening in July 1968. The room was packed with other media representatives, including the aforementioned celebrity. I was allowed to interview Mr Armstrong first and did so from a squatting position in front of him while he sat on a bed. I read through the questions in sequence and Mr Armstrong replied effusively, apparently in the belief that I knew what I was asking about. I then came to the final question, which did seem to me a little odd, but as I hadn't understood most of the previous questions I assumed it had some hidden (from me) significance.

There was a gasp of astonishment among my media colleagues when I asked it and a distinct tsk, tsking from Mr Bowman, who was there in connection with the Rodney Rice programme or some other adventure. I had asked the celebrated black musician, 'How come you have such great big white teeth?' He looked astonished and then pityingly at me. He broke the few seconds of embarrassed silence with the response, 'I bite my wife regularly on the back.'

I didn't understand the reply either, and as I left Mr Bowman was tsk, tsking away.

# JOHN BRUTON

My most embarrassing moment was when I discovered that I had failed to reply to Seán Power's very reasonable request to recall an embarrassing moment, scratched my head furiously, thought back to my schooldays, back to my teenage years, and over my whole political career — and just drew a blank. I am actually embarrassed to discover that I can think of no embarrassing moment. I hope this does not mean that I have no shame!

# BISHOP JOHN BUCKLEY

I was born in west Cork, and sport — in particular hurling, football and bowling — was always very much part of our lives. It was something that was bred in our bones and entwined in our lives. In national school we were very fortunate that we had a local teacher who had a passionate interest in sport, and he encouraged us in every way to develop our sporting talents. In fact, we thought that sport was part of the primary school curriculum because of the importance which he attached to it. I still have vivid recollections of under-12 and under-13 games against neighbouring schools in west Cork, and the grim determination and boundless energy of our team. The Siege of Troy and the Battle of Waterloo were only minor events by comparison.

> With skill superb
> the sliotar will be hit,
> clean and clear to the keen eye
> sweet-sounding to the well-tuned ear.

Later on in boarding school in Cork city, where hurling was the dominant game, we were given every opportunity to develop our skills further. A frequent visitor to the college was the late and beloved Christy Ring, whose memory will for ever remain indelible in the annals of the sporting history of Cork. I continued to improve at the game, and I achieved my main objective of captaining the college Harty team. The Harty Cup is the most prestigious trophy in Munster colleges hurling. A place on the Cork Minor hurling team was the realisation of a dream for me. I then decided to study for the priesthood, and attended the university and seminary in Maynooth. Rules at that time were very strict. We were not allowed to leave the college to participate in sport with our local club. Our sporting activities were limited to the holiday period of three months during the summer. Needless to say, we made the most of it, and I will elaborate.

A friend of mine, and a great player, Gerard Creedon from Inchigeela, and myself, received invitations from various hurling clubs to play with them during the summer season. According to the rules of the GAA we could only play with one club, but we accepted all invitations, fully realising the risk of suspension if they found out about our surreptitious activities. The various clubs we played for were widely scattered, and communication in those days between club officers was practically non-existent.

We survived unnoticed for two years, having played with as many as eight clubs. Eventually our luck ran out in the most embarrassing circumstances possible.

Both of us were invited to participate in a seminar on the ideals of the GAA in the west Cork town of Dunmanway, with whom we had played, as they naturally thought, legally! We were on the panel and had answered some questions on the ideals of the GAA and, in particular, on the whole question of discipline and respect for the rules. Then someone in the audience produced that evening's newspaper, the *Cork Evening Echo*, and he read from the banner headlines of the sporting page: 'Journeymen Hurlers Suspended by Cork County Board'. The various clubs we had played with were featured in the article, some of whom had representatives at the seminar. I said to Gerard that we had better get Garda protection on our way out, because the clubs with whom we had played were also fined. I still turn purple when I think of it. We were asked for a response. I made what I consider the greatest speech ever from the dock! I spoke about our love for sport, for hurling in particular, the short summer holiday, and the few opportunities available to us to play hurling. I also spoke of our desire to promote the game in every way at our disposal, and that meant helping struggling clubs! My words struck a chord, because we got back safely to our home village of Inchigeela without police protection!

# MIKE BURNS

*Flagrante!*

Location: the Imperial Hotel, Castlebar, circa early 1960s.

And it started out innocently enough.

A late-night dinner and a libation or two of wine after a long day's filming (official opening of Tynagh

Mines in County Galway, plus a feature on Fr Tom Egan's restoration plans/hopes for Ballintubber Abbey, near Castlebar, Co. Mayo).

Frank Hall would be more than pleased: his RTE 'Newsbeat' programme would be the richer.

As I said, innocent enough. Until we (the cameraman, Stuart Hetherington, the sound recordist, Fintan Ryan, and mise) decided to have a well-earned digestive in the hotel bar.

Within minutes we were joined by the hotel owner, the editor of the *Connaught Telegraph* and other local luminaries. The weather and crops, the tall tales of the West, the fishing exploits of Sean Lemass and Charlie Forte . . . all provided suitable conversational ploys.

As the clock ticked, the wise camera crew departed for bed. I (unfortunately and not for the first or last time) stayed on.

Long after the midnight hour I repaired to bed, to find that I had left my pyjamas in the camera car, far too late to invade the camera crew's golden sleep for the car keys. A night in the buff was in prospect. But, before heading for dreamland, a visit to the down-the-corridor bathroom was in order.

Cautious but swift exit from bedroom (nothing *en suite* about the Imperial). No sign of life. Rapid visit to the facilities, followed by further hasty return to my bedroom. Except it wasn't — my bedroom, that is.

Instead, I found myself in a well-lit bedroom where a couple were engaging in what the decorous tabloid newspapers gently refer to as 'sexual exploits'. In the best *News of the World* tradition, I made an apologetic 'Oops! Sorry' noise and rapidly departed.

Back in my room the sleepless agonising began. I could even visualise the newspaper headlines: 'RTE Newsman caught *flagrante* in Mayo hotel'. So, shortly after 6 a.m. I woke the camera crew and said: 'Let's get the hell out of here and I'll explain why later.'

Within minutes we were on our way to Pontoon — but not before I had checked the hotel register to find out whose privacy I had invaded.

With mounting horror I read the entry of a *very* senior foreign diplomat and his wife.

Weeks followed days of fearful revelation. But there was no enquiry, no protest about the nude invader. Eventually the senior diplomat thankfully departed for another far-foreign post — and I breathed more happily.

The years roll forward. Michael O'Kennedy is now Foreign Minister and we meet at an embassy reception.

The Minister, gentleman that he was and is, expansively invited me to join his conversation with an all-too-familiar figure — visiting Dublin again after years of overseas service. We were introduced and within minutes someone had grabbed the Minister's arm and steered him towards another group.

'Don't believe we've had the pleasure of meeting before,' the diplomat said.

I thought it was now time for honesty.

'As a matter of fact, we have,' I said, and proceeded to recall the night in the Imperial Hotel.

Amazingly, the diplomat didn't lash out. Instead, he looked furtively about and responded: 'If you don't mind, if you don't mention that incident to my wife, I certainly won't.'

Never did find out who the 'other woman' was . . .

# GAY BYRNE

On the corner of our street was a little shop called Monaghan's. Mr Monaghan displayed his fruit on a stand outside the front door of his shop. Asking for it.

Little Gaybo in his short pants was 5 years old and could

not resist temptation. Egged on by my pal Tommy Heffernan, I nicked an apple from the display. I was naive enough to walk cheerfully into our house, munching on the forbidden fruit.

My mother pounced immediately. 'Where did you get that apple?' I lied that someone had given it to me. I might as well have saved my breath to cool my porridge. My mother could spot a lie at fifty paces. Clutching my precious piggy bank, in the shape of a red tin pillar-box, I was frog-marched back up the street to Monaghan's. The shop was full, bursting, it seemed, with people, all of whom stopped what they were doing to hear my mother ask in stentorian tones: 'Mr Monaghan, have you got apples on your stand outside?'

'Yes, Mrs Byrne.'

'I have to report to you that this *person* (withering contempt) has stolen an apple from your stand. This is the very apple, Mr Monaghan.'

Christy Monaghan, who twigged immediately what she was at, as did everyone else in the shop, threw up his hands in shock. Everyone stopped breathing.

'Did you know this, Mr Monaghan?'

(Gravely) 'No, I didn't, Mrs Byrne.'

'Well, he did. And now he must make *restitution*! Here is his savings bank.' (the miserable thing clanked treacherously). 'You must take it.' (High drama and handing over of the piggy bank, in the manner of Clare Bow renouncing Gary Cooper at the height of her melodramatic despair.)

I started to cry, the loud wails falling into the depths of the accusing silence in the shop, as Christy Monaghan fetched a knife and laboriously inserted it into the small oblong slot at the top of the red pillar-box. Slowly, as slowly as the coming of Christmas, down the blade of the knife slid one, two, three of my precious pennies. I howled more loudly.

They were not going to let me off that lightly. Everyone in the shop felt it was their bounden duty to give me a lecture and to tsk tsk over the state of the world. What was it coming to when an honest man could not leave his apples outside his front door! What were boys coming to these days? And Mrs Byrne having reared such a nice, such a good, such an *honest* family! That was, up to this moment . . .

Then I had to place the apple butt on Mr Monaghan's counter before slinking out of the shop like a whipped dog, all eyes still boring into me, forlorn little Gaybo, shame written along his back, having to walk very burning step back home.

I never stole another apple.

# MONICA CARR
*A Thing of the Past*

One of the admittedly few advantages of having clocked up the years, I have discovered, is the disappearance of embarrassment. Like the halcyon days of youth, when limbs were supple and rheumaticky twinges unknown and we were subject to moments of acute, exquisite embarrassment, it is all a dream.

When the miracle happened is unknown. Like Topsy, in *Uncle Tom's Cabin*, I 'spect it just growed.

Nowadays we know that nothing like that really matters. Even if we are the talk of the town today, appearing in the district court for not paying your bills, or driving recklessly, we are comfortingly aware that it will be ancient history tomorrow. It almost, I swear, makes up for the creaky knees and forgetting people's names.

To this day, however, I never excuse myself in company to make a 'comfort stop' without remembering a teenage picnic in the thirties.

My late sister and I were invited to visit two boys who were making local history by living in a tent on the banks of the Liffey from April to September — an unthinkable thing to attempt at the time in our conservative community and we were wildly eager to see the set-up with our own eyes.

A cycle of more than twelve miles to the venue was a 'piece of cake' in 'them thar' days, except that in our excitement we forgot essentials like the need to answer calls of nature before meeting up with the lads.

Shall I ever forget the torture of that afternoon and evening by the Liffey? Incredibly, we stuck it out, but didn't finish the tin mugs of tea we were offered before the homeward journey.

The other embarrassing moment of youth was the annual pilgrimage of transporting our family turkey hen to the station cock in the next parish.

Wartime meant Shanks's mare or the bike. Only the doctor and the priest had petrol for their cars.

Full of myself — like teenagers the world over — and very conscious of boys, of course, the idea of cycling through the village with the bird on the carrier, securely tied down in her box with yards of binder twine on which my father insisted, I had to pass the usual group of corner-boys in the village street.

That wretched bird never ever failed to poke her long gangling head out of the hession wrappings as I sailed past, evoking, of course, the usual catcalls and whistles, and I died a small death, but there was no other route to that turkey cock station.

Ridiculous, when you think back, but that is how it was.

# NED CASH

(as told to Des Maguire*)

*How I almost never became 'King of the Horse Dealers'*

My developing career as a horse dealer was almost cut short prematurely outside Kilrush, Co. Clare, when I was around 18 years of age. The family caravan was then based in Sallins, a few miles outside Naas, and one day I decided to head off for Kilrush fair by bicycle.

I planned to spend the night in Fanny O'Dea's pub and lodging house halfway between Kilrush and Ennis. When I arrived in Fanny O'Dea's, however, I was told that the Kilrush fair had been put back for a few days which was terrible news altogether. It was too late to head home, so I had some supper and asked the lady of the house if there was a dance on anywhere in the locality that night.

She went out to the pub to ask the lads and came back with the news that there would be a dance later on about six miles away in a house called Ryan's. She directed me to Ryan's and I set off on the bike.

The journey took me across a maze of backroads in bleak and wild country. On the way I passed by a quarry and noticed a number of men walking around the pit face. I thought it was strange for a group of men to be in a quarry so late at night, but didn't stop to find out what they were doing. I had great difficulty finding Ryan's and the dance was in full swing by the time I eventually tracked it down. It was a good dance, as country dances went in those days, and although I chatted up a number of girls, I didn't get off my mark.

I left Ryan's around two o'clock in the morning and, needless to say, it was pitch black. After I had been cycling for around half an hour I had a feeling I was going astray, but unfortunately there wasn't a sinner on the road to ask directions. There was nothing for it but to cycle on.

I saw a light in a house across a field and thought that my luck was in, that it had to be Fanny O'Dea's. I parked the bike by the side of the ditch and walked across the field towards the light.

As I approached the house I realised it wasn't Fanny O'Dea's, but I thought I had better look for directions all the same — despite the lateness of the hour. I knocked on the half-door and a very nice lady came out.

'Good night, mam,' I said.

'Good night, garsun. You're out late.'

'I'm looking for Fanny O'Dea's.'

'Oh, you're miles out of your way. How are you travelling?'

'I left my bike by the ditch down at the road. What am I going to do? Is there any chance you could put me up for the night?'

'I don't think so,' she said. 'Come on in anyway and have a cup of tea.'

She soon put a big mug of steaming sweet tea in front of me and two buttered slices of home-made soda bread.

'It's clear you'll never make Fanny O'Dea's tonight,' she said. 'I tell you what. I have no room in the bedroom for you, but if you like you can sleep in the kitchen here in front of the hearth until morning.'

'Oh, that would be great, mam,' I said.

She went into a bedroom and got some blankets for me and we made up a makeshift bed in front of the hearth. I finished off the tea and soda bread and settled down in the bed.

After a while she went back down to the bedroom and I could hear a number of voices whispering.

'God, you know this young fellow might do the job rightly,' one of the voices said.

'Oh Pat, don't,' I could hear the woman reply. 'He's only a garsun that's lost and jaded.'

'Shut up, woman. He'll do all right,' the man she called Pat said, walking into the kitchen, closely followed by four other big heavy men. I hadn't noticed any of them when I was talking to the woman in the kitchen earlier, so I was very worried, not knowing what to expect.

'Come on now,' Pat said, giving me a kick or two to get me on my feet. 'We want you to come with us.'

'I don't want to go anywhere,' I said, growing more frightened by the minute.

'Come on,' he said again, pulling me out the door into the yard where the other men collected shovels, spades, a bucket and a rope.

They pushed me in front of them across a number of fields and ditches until we came to an old graveyard. They brought me to a grave, gave me a spade, and we started to dig away there in the early hours of the morning.

Then they put a rope around my waist, lowered me into the grave and gave me a shovel with a short handle and the bucket. I kept filling the bucket and they would take it up and empty it. Some time later I felt a board and knew I had come upon a coffin. Then my feet went right through the coffin and I called out: 'Oh God, men, pull me up. Pull me up.'

'You're all right,' Pat replied. 'Take the boards off the coffin.'

I lifted the boards and could see the rotten body of an old woman and the stench was foul.

'Right,' said Pat, 'on that person's neck there is a gold necklace and there are two diamond rings on her fingers. Bring them up.'

When I went to pull off the first ring, the flesh came too. It was the worst thing that had ever happened to me in my life. The second ring brought flesh off with it too.

'In the name of God, pull me up,' I called again.

'As soon as you have the necklace off,' said Pat.

I rooted around and saw a lovely gold necklace around the neck of the corpse.

'How am I going to get it off?' I asked them.

'Put your hand around the back of her neck and you will

find the clasp and keep at it until you open it,' Pat called down.

I rooted for the clip, but couldn't find it anywhere. I started to lift up her head and the whole scalp came away rotten. Oh God, this is terrible, I thought, but try as I might I couldn't get the necklace off. Every time I put my hand around her neck my fingers would sink into the rotten flesh and I would squirm. Finally, I kept pulling at the necklace until it broke open, and sent the two rings and the necklace up in the bucket to the men. I was waiting for them to pull me up when I heard them arguing among themselves.

'Nobody knows about this only ourselves, and if this boy is allowed away free he will talk, so we had better put him down under,' one of the voices was saying.

'Oh, please don't do that,' I called up. 'I swear I'll tell nobody about this.'

I could hear one of them say to Pat and the others. 'God, men, don't do it. We have what we came for.' He came closer to the edge of the grave and I could see his face clearly. He had a worried look.

'Look,' he said. 'You heard them talking yourself. They are planning to shoot you and leave you in that grave.'

'Oh, God, don't do that,' I begged.

'OK, make me a promise then,' he said. 'Get down on your knees there and swear to God that nobody will know of this.'

The irony of kneeling down in a desecrated grave in the middle of the morning and swearing to God that I would keep my mouth shut about a grave robbery escaped me.

'I swear to God,' I said.

The men pulled me up and we covered in the grave. Then we walked silently back through the fields to the house. The woman who had given me the tea was waiting in the yard for us, and I could see that she was relieved to see me back with the men. Daylight was breaking by this time, and they were anxious to be rid of me before it became too bright.

Pat walked me down to where I had left the bike, brought

me to a crossroads and gave me directions for Fanny O'Dea's. I could hear blasting in the quarry as I cycled away from the house, and I thought for a moment they had changed their minds about letting me off alive.

I didn't look back till I reached Fanny O'Dea's and nearly knocked the door down in my rush to get in.

The woman of the house came down in her nightie and opened the door. 'Oh, it's you,' she said. 'My God, what's the smell?'

'I stumbled into a pig sty,' I said.

I went straight upstairs to the bathroom. I ran the bath and got in and got out, back in and out again, rubbing and scrubbing myself to try and get rid of the smell.

I went down then for breakfast and had a cup of tea. There were a number of people already in the dining-room and they were disgusted at the smell which was still on my clothes.

On my way home I stopped off in Ennis and bought a new set of clothes and boots. I went into a hotel, had another bath and changed my clothes. Then I headed back for Sallins.

Two weeks later, all my hair fell out in what was obviously a delayed reaction to the shock of being forced to get down into a grave and rob a corpse. I hadn't a screed of hair left on my head.

Oh, bejaney, I'm properly done for now. Nobody will look at me. I'll have no chance with the women at all now, I kept saying over and over to myself.

My hair gradually came back in black patches, and the next thing it turned snow white. The whole family wondered what happened at Kilrush that made me go bald first and later snow white, but I never told a sinner until now about my early morning escapade in the County Clare graveyard.

* From *Horses Are My Life — The Ned Cash Story* by Des Maguire, Agri-Books © Des Maguire.

# PETER CASSELLS

Over the years, everybody of a certain political persuasion claims that their relatives were in the GPO in 1916. Whatever about this claim, I believed every Meath and Dublin follower who, after a few pints, claimed that they were in Croke Park for all three of the famous Leinster finals won eventually by Meath.

There were a number of minor embarrassments at all three matches. The sight, on the first day, of Mick Lyons frying fish fingers and heating beans two hours before the match, as he helped Joe Cassells feed his six hungry children, made me despair. How could such a softie strike terror into the Dublin forwards on that day.

At the second match, we squirmed as a young couple, on what was obviously their first day in Croke Park, asked a crowd already angry at the lack of tickets, 'Are there numbers on those seats or can we sit anywhere?' The same crowd made sure I felt the embarrassment at half-time as sandwiches from some of my Dublin friends were passed along the row of seats with the message, 'Your mother asked us to give ya these.'

However, these were minor compared to my most embarrassing moment during the third match. Early on in the game, as Dublin forward, Niall Guiden, skinned Meath half-back Kevin Foley, I roared, 'For Jaysus sake, Kevin, let him know you're there.' Meath fans will know what was required. As Guiden scored another brilliant point, I told Foley to get the lead out of his arse. Later in the second half, as Dublin got on top, I told everyone around me, 'I always knew Kevin Foley was no use. He should never have been picked.' I implored the selectors at the top of my voice, 'Take Foley off before we are destroyed.'

And then the miracle occurred. As we entered injury time, with Dublin three points up, Kevin Foley got the ball near his own goal. Three passes later, he was in the Dublin half where he planted the ball in the back of the Dublin net. In the excitement, I threw my arms around the woman in the Meath scarf in front of me. The crowd around me began to congratulate her. 'Mrs Foley, Kevin is a genius.' 'What a goal!' 'Best player Meath had today.' 'You should be proud of your son.'

As I slunk away, I wondered if those who know my capacity for enjoying myself would, years later, believe that that really was my most embarrassing moment.

# SEAN CLARKIN

*Ears that Hear, Mouths that Speak, Eyes that See!*

My father should have known better. During dinner he made the fatal mistake of not only having an adult conversation, but of diverting the final sentence towards his offspring.

'He's a bloody fool, that man! Tell him that too!' — his head inclined towards us. 'DUTY' in big letters began to flash inside my brain.

Midday: a child (me), burdened with too many dictates, lumbers reluctantly but conscientiously towards the teacher I would afterwards describe in one of my poems as 'fat for his age and interested in roses'.

'Sir . . . my daddy says . . !' Overweight he may have been, but once he survived that test he was destined to live to retire. In keeping with the times, he never revealed how damaged his self-image was. His wife looked at me peculiarly until she died.

I carried a report home to the distraught general. So young and so burdened with duties! That's how I remember childhood. My older brother, though of a different calibre, likewise. It was I who proved a fool in the schoolyard. And afterwards . . !

That teacher and my father were active members of the INTO! How things were patched up, no one knows. Mum won't tell. And the other three of the two partnerships are now dead. It may not have been the only time his child psychology let him down, just the most embarrassing.

Myself, I've been embarrassed too. We were on holiday in Courtown Harbour where my father was born. We were camping itinerant style: a caravan or two, a tent or two. We usually camped in a field behind the beach at Duffcarraig, where the traders from Gorey tipped up their carts along the margins of the lane and let the horses graze during the midweek lazy afternoons when traders still did such things. It was the 'Well field' and an endless procession of water-seekers would harmlessly tread a path past the guy ropes of the tents. Never a thing was touched though we were often miles away.

The lady who owned the field also had a big old-fashioned house where she kept guests. One of these spelt mystery: he drove a huge Jaguar. It was parked on the neat gravel. A jar of human eyes occupied the back window, five or six eyes in a liquid. Sometimes they floated about, peeping in or out.

We were into boating and we had what I knew was a magnificent clinker-built boat that needed endless scraping and dragging. I never knew, or don't know now in any case, how the man with the Jag got invited to come for a trip in the Waterwag. Perhaps it was to do with the fact that, like the Jag, there was something unique about our boat.

The highlight of the day, I thought, would be the trip to the harbour with the eyes! Not so. Out at sea, it was quite normal for us to be resourceful. This meant, at times, the centre-board casing acting as a urinal. It was a casual arrangement, not unlike our camping arrangement for the men, when a little trench was dug and a sod replaced each time. This big Englishman with the eyes on the back window added solemnity to the occasion. Perhaps it was not only eyes he surgeoned! Could I risk exposing it?

The sea basked in its beauty. Little eddies of waves washed against the gunwale and the gulls came to look. They'd seen it all before, except for the man. The very English man.

Little eddies of liquid trickled down my legs. Hot liquid. Inside, and — I looked down — outside my short pants.

He must have been a cool, kind man after all. He showed no signs of noticing anything, even my embarrassment! Perhaps he only cut out people's eyes when they were damaged beyond repair, but how was I to know before? On the other hand, a surgeon that didn't notice things could be dangerous! Even then, I was learning that you can't win.

As I left the Jag, I noticed that at least four of the eyes were staring down at the upholstery where I'd been sitting! As I looked, I knew that I was looking with more than two eyes. That must be why I can see the wet patch still, whenever I think about it.

# PADDY COLE

I suppose one of my most embarrassing moments happened in Castleblaney some years back when I was running our family pub and restaurant. We used to have a Monday night jazz session which became so popular that the place was packed. I used to play with the band and run the bar as well. One Monday I was very late arriving at the bar from my house. I had my musical instruments and the bar float money all under my arms on the way through the door. The place was so packed I was finding it difficult to make my way through the crowd. My eldest son, Pearse, met me, and was in the process of telling me *in no uncertain manner* how late I was and how stuck they were for the float.

At that moment a fellow shouted, 'How are you, Paddy?' I didn't know him (still don't), but he had his feet up on the velvet chair in front of him. 'Get your f—— feet off that seat', I replied, and walked on. I did notice the hurt and disappointment on his face, but I was under pressure and just went for him.

Later, we started to play the music, and I saw the same guy going to the toilet, on crutches. He was an invalid. I was devastated. I had a long chat with him later and sorted everything out. He was a lovely guy and, like I said, I don't even know his name. That was easily one of my most embarrassing moments!

(This is an excerpt from Tim Ryan's book on the life of Paddy Cole, *Tell Roy Rogers I'm not in.*)

# STEPHEN COLLINS

*The Day I Set Fire to a Launderette in Chicago*

S tanding in the middle of a blazing launderette on the south side of Chicago, numbly waiting for the police to arrive to question me about the cause of the fire, is something I can now look back on with a rueful smile; but it wasn't funny at the time.

It all started simply enough. As a student I spent one summer working in Chicago, staying with my aunt and uncle in the pleasant suburb of Oaklawn. I got a handy job with the local schools board painting and renovating schools during the summer holidays. The jobs were reserved for local students as part of some FÁS-type scheme, but in good old Mayor Daly's Chicago, being Irish automatically qualified me. One of the jobs involved putting fresh tar on a leaky roof. In the 100° heat it was hard work and in the process my overalls became encrusted with tar.

'You had better soak them in gasoline. There's no point trying to wash them', said my Aunt Noreen.

I dutifully stuffed the overalls into a big plastic bucket and filled it with petrol which is ridiculously cheap in the US. A day later there was some improvement, but not much.

'The best thing you can do now is take them down to the laundromat. I am not going to put them in my washing machine', she told me.

I tipped the petrol-soaked overalls into a plastic bag and walked down to the laundromat (the American for launderette). I unthinkingly tipped the contents of the plastic bag into a washing machine, set the controls and sat down to read a book while the job was being done.

The launderette was full of women chatting and gossiping while waiting for their washing. I quickly became absorbed in my book, but after a few minutes became aware that a bit of commotion was going on.

'Can you smell gasoline?' said one woman loudly.

'Gee, the smell is overpowering. What the heck is going on?' replied her friend.

'Where's the supervisor?' asked another nervously, getting to her feet.

I was quickly jolted back to reality. Sure enough, there was an overwhelming smell of petrol and I had no doubt what the source was. Nobody else in the launderette knew where it was coming from, but I was immediately oppressed by a feeling of guilt and apprehension as I tried to look unconcerned. As the women got to their feet and demanded in raucous tones to know what was happening, there was a sudden explosion.

The lid of my washing machine flew into the air. Flames poured out of the top, licking their way along the line of throbbing machines. The women screamed and stampeded for the door as smoke filled the air. The alarm went off and the manager suddenly materialised, and he too bolted for the door.

I stupidly stood my ground as the smoke swirled around me. Feeling responsible for the débâcle, I shuffled around the building making sure nobody else was left inside. Like a captain going down with the ship, I felt I had no option but to be last off the premises. Gradually the smoke cleared. The manager returned with a fire extinguisher which he turned on the flames still shooting from my washing machine. The fire brigade turned up and hoses were unfurled, but by the time they were ready to fight the fire it was under control.

Apart from blackened and singed paintwork along the row of washing machines there was no great harm done, but I waited in trepidation to take my medicine, fully convinced of my guilt and only thankful that I hadn't incinerated a harmless group of women doing their washing.

I overheard the firemen calling the police and felt that all I could do was wait until they arrived and own up.

The manager suddenly approached me, but before I could babble out a confession he apologised profusely and commended my courage in staying put to make sure everybody got out safely. 'Sir, I would like to offer you compensation for damage to your clothing. That machine,' he said, pointing to the offending object, 'has been giving trouble for a while. An electrical fault has been giving problems, but it never caused a fire like this before.'

Beginning to breathe more easily, I recovered my composure. So it hadn't really been my fault after all, even if I had unwittingly poured petrol on the sparking machine.

Graciously declining the offer of compensation, I removed my soggy overalls from the washing tub, put them back into their petrol-smelling plastic bag and left quickly, just as the police car pulled to a stop outside the launderette. Restraining the impulse to run, I walked rapidly away. Maybe it wasn't all my fault, but I certainly didn't feel like explaining myself to the Chicago police.

# JIM CONNOLLY

In the sixties I was a member of the Monarchs showband in Limerick city. These were the days of the large ballrooms all over Ireland and bands like the Monarchs travelled the length and breadth of the country, often as many as five nights a week. Dancing was the big social occasion and crowds of a thousand people and more were not uncommon. Nowadays, with discos and luxury bars, it is difficult to imagine the popularity of large cold dancehalls with no bar facilities. However, that was the way it was and it forms the background to the very embarrassing moment I am about to relate.

Our band was in the middle of a very busy period in the winter of 1962/63. The normal Sunday and midweek dancing was increased almost everywhere by formal dress dances as clubs and business firms held their annual social events. Some time after Christmas our drummer Frank caught a heavy flu and couldn't travel with us to play in Mitchelstown, Co. Cork. Our stand-by drummer, a very talented and obliging young man (whom I will only refer to as R. as he later tragically died in his early thirties) was available and willing to travel.

Everything went smoothly in Mitchelstown until the interval, when bands usually took a short break. Dancing continued, however, throughout the interval (bands used to split in two, with one half remaining to keep things going while the other half left the stage). On this occasion, I was on stage playing the piano supported by our bass player and our stand-in drummer.

I was the leader of the Monarchs and normally played the trumpet; I also made whatever announcements were to be made into one of the several microphones standing in front of the band. It was common during intervals for musicians to change instruments — that's why I was playing the piano, which was to one side of the large stage and a good bit away from any standing microphone.

I should say at this stage that, apart from his drumming, R. was also an excellent singer, and we were always delighted to add his songs to our programme whenever he played with us. On the night in question R. had a mike close to his face as he played the interval with me, and he sang a number of songs one after the other. When we had finished the set of three dances to an appreciative crowd, I turned my head back from my seat at the piano and called to R. to announce the next dance. He could do this into the mike without leaving the drums, whilst I would have had to walk to the centre of the stage to do it, so it was just an automatic common sense request on my part.

I sat back on my chair at the piano and relaxed for a moment before it dawned on me that no announcement had been made and that the dancers were still on the floor waiting expectantly for something to happen. Thinking that R. hadn't heard me over the applause I quickly turned to him again and repeated my request for him to announce the next dance. Once again I relaxed and let my mind drift, only to be jolted back to reality after perhaps a minute or two by the realisation that the dancers were still on the floor looking up at us.

This time I turned sharply to R. only to see him red faced, trying in vain to get the words out. Oh my God, I thought. What have I done to poor R? How utterly thoughtless of me! I had completely forgotten that he suffered from an extremely bad stammer and that the only time when words flowed effortlessly from him was when he sang.

I immediately walked to the nearest mike and made the announcement myself and, of course, the moment passed.

I know full well that R. didn't hold it against me that I had landed him in what must have been a few minutes of excruciating embarrassment for him as he struggled without success to make the announcement. He knew that his stammer had just momentarily slipped my mind. Also, of course, living with a stammer was part of his everyday existence.

For my part, I can honestly say that my slip-up was probably the most embarrassing moment of my adult life, even though it was perhaps understandable after R. had just sung several songs so effortlessly and so well.

Probably most of the hurts caused by people in their personal lives are through thoughtlessness — forgotten birthdays or anniversaries or a kind word from time to time. The major things we get involved in during our lives and which occupy so much of our minds and our time may not be as important to other people as they are to us. We should always bear that in mind.

# SISTER M. CONSILIO

### A Pot Pourri of Faux-Pas

*'O wad some power the giftie gie us
to see ourselves as others see us.'*

S ome years ago, I was invited by the health authority to sit on a selection board to make new appointments in the field of alcoholism treatment. The occasion demanded that I should be smart and formal. In those times, for a nun, a spotless black habit and starched white hat was the order of the day. I had only one, made by myself, and no longer pristine. Accordingly, the hat was in the wash, and the habit rolled up ready to be cleaned on the day before the session I was due to attend.

At noon the phone rang. The interviews were already in progress in the boardroom. What was the delay? My presence was expected at once! I had mistaken the day! Panic! Putting on the wet hat and the crumpled habit, I waylaid a priest friend and his companion, who were just off on a fishing trip. To their inconvenience, but evident amusement, we set off at speed in their car for the mental hospital some miles away. Worse was to come. On the way, it became evident that not only was my habit rather dishevelled, it was actually falling apart. My slip was going to be showing literally as well as metaphorically!

High-speed emergency repairs were carried out with the aid of fishing line and the skill and inventiveness of the anglers. Speed limits were flouted, and in record time we were at the hospital.

I arrived breathless, dodged surprised-looking orderlies and took my place in the boardroom — a most unusual-looking nun amongst a bemused panel of psychology experts. Steam still rose from my freshly washed, still wet cap, giving a whole new meaning to the notion of a 'drying out unit'! Assorted salmon flies were attached to my black habit, precariously holding together its disintegrating parts. What the senior psychiatrist made of it, history does not record; perhaps for him it was all in a day's work!

What I do remember is that by the end of the afternoon the most suitable candidates had been appointed. As so often happens in my experience, the objective was achieved, if in circumstances quite other than I had planned.

Usually it is with the best will in the world that we inadvertently lay these 'banana skins' for ourselves. Like the doctor of psychiatry, I recall two doctors of divinity whose first encounters with me may have caused them a little puzzlement, to say the least.

On one occasion the local bishop came to visit Cuan Mhuire house that was only recently up and running. To get everything shipshape, we had stored away all the clutter in my bedroom. After being shown all around, the bishop expressed himself delighted with the set-up. What inspired him, I wondered afterwards, to add, 'I seem to have seen everywhere except your own living quarters.' The door of my room was pushed open with difficulty. It revealed — to his bewilderment, and my chagrin — piled high to the ceiling with every object imaginable, what was evidently the dwelling place of a kleptomaniac!

More recently, at another of our houses, we had some

distinguished guests coming to join us for a meal. Just beforehand, I met a black-suited stranger in the hallway, who seemed a little lost. I was helpfully suggesting to him that perhaps he had come to the wrong place, maybe he had an appointment elsewhere in the neighbourhood, when it suddenly dawned on me that he was the bishop, and I myself had indeed invited him to come on that day and had completely forgotten about it! Despite this minor hiccup, I'm glad to say that the lunch party was enjoyed by all concerned.

Such moments are certainly rather deflating, but when all is said and done, they simply show us that we're human. The discomfort quickly fades, leaving only pleasurable memories of fate's comic interludes. On balance, I'm glad of them all, and I hope that other people who have been embroiled in my moments of aberration have gained from them amusement, insights — on occasion, perhaps even a free lunch! — but never any lasting hurt.

# TIMMY CONWAY

*Round Pound Accounting*

The death of Gerrard Sweetman resulted in the Kildare by-election of 1970. I put my name forward to contest the convention to be the candidate for the Labour Party. It was more to test the waters, as at that time I was more interested in qualifying as an accountant than running for politics. Joe Birmingham was determined to be the candidate. Joe saw me as a threat and someone he would have to keep a close eye on.

During the election campaign I was Director of Finance. When the votes were counted, Joe Birmingham's vote ensured that, come the next general election, a Labour candidate would be returned as deputy for Kildare. Like any successful politician, it was incumbent on him to establish himself as the candidate and get rid of any would-be suitors.

Joe chose the battlefield: the review of the election. The venue was the Town Hall in Naas and it was on the Sunday after the election result. Joe brought all his supporters from the south and as I saw the hall fill up, I knew that something was afoot.

I had to present the financial statement for the by-election. At that time I was working in Irish Ropes as an assistant accountant. In that company we had a very progressive and new method of accounting technique. This was called round pound accounting. It was simple and effective and it cut out all shillings and pence and presented the figures in pounds only. A figure of £3. 17s. 6d was rounded up to £4, while a figure of £4. 3s. 4d was rounded down to £4. In the end it all balanced and made it easier for someone to read a set of accounts.

I presented the accounts for the Kildare by-election using this system, and had it photocopied and circulated to the people present. These were two vital mistakes.

I called out the contribution from the Ballitore branch of £8 and the contribution of the Athy branch of £12. I showed in detail where the money came from, and where it went to. When I had finished there was a scattering of applause which I thought rather unfair after all the work that had gone into this and the fine result we had achieved. I sat down and called for queries on the accounts. A member from the Ballitore branch put up his hand and said: 'The Ballitore branch paid in £8. 7s. 6d and it is down on this paper as £8. I want to know where the seven shillings and six pence went?' This was immediately followed by a delegate from the Athy branch asking the same question. I said that although they had paid in the amounts stated, I had rounded them down using the system of round pound accounting. This was to make the report easier to understand. The money had been lodged and, taking all of the pluses and minuses into consideration, the accounts were correct to the nearest pound. There were howls from the southern branches, but it was left to Joe Birmingham to articulate the sentiment of his disciples. Joe stood up and called on the chair to allow him to speak. He commenced his speech in the way he has always done, as follows.

'Friends. We have had an excellent general election and I am sure that when it comes to the next general election we will take the seat for the Labour Party.' This was accompanied by shouts of enthusiasm and congratulations from all sides. 'Friends', he continued, 'it will not be done by incompetence and new fandangled ideas brought in by the new gurus of the Labour Party, Conor Cruise O'Brien, David Thornley, and the man sitting up there, Justin Keating. As to my young friend, Timmy Conway, and his new fandangled ideas of round pound accounting, I would have this to say to him. 'You can take these new fandangled ideas up to Trinity College where they belong, but do not introduce them to the ordinary plain people of Kildare. I would like to address myself to the two questions that were asked from the Ballitore branch and the Athy branch. The Ballitore branch paid in £8. 7s. 6d and it is down here for £8. The Athy branch paid in £12. 4s. 5d and it is down for £12. I want to know where the 7/6 and the 4/5 went to?'

I stood up and said that although the money was in the bank I accounted for it in round pound accounting.

At this Joe went into high gear and said: 'I am not accusing that man there of embezzling 7/6 and 4/5. I am an ordinary plain Kildare man and I cannot understand this new fandangled thing they call round pound accounting. I demand that an apology be made to the branches concerned for this débâcle.' This was accompanied by a loud burst of applause.

The meeting degenerated into a slagging match, with members jumping up and accusing me of bringing the Labour Party into disrepute. One delegate accused me of embezzling the money; another accused me of bringing communist ideas into the Labour Party; and yet another accused me of being a capitalist and that there was no place in the Labour Party for accountants as they were up the bosses' arses. All in all, Joe managed to annihilate me. I did not attend another constituency meeting for at least five months.

It was game, set and match to Joe Birmingham. Joe went on to win the Labour seat at the next general election, and afterwards he became my best friend.

# EOGHAN CORRY
## *Theatre Festival Farce*

On the opening night of the 1994 Dublin Theatre Festival the *Irish Press*, whose boards at the time I trod in the lonely position of arts editor, carried a review of a play which had never taken place.

The simplest explanation of what happened is that one of our first-time reviewers came back to the newspaper and panicked, thinking she had gone to the wrong play.

Names are significant here. The play she went to see was called *Hanging Around*, and while she was hanging around there she thought she should have been at *The Comeback* (in the adjoining theatre in Andrew's Lane). She returned to the newsroom trembling with fear for her imagined faux-pas, got together some pre-play publicity for the other play from her notes, and made up the review, lock, stock and curtains.

The situation got rapidly worse while I was oblivious to all of this, tripping the 'dark fantastic' in the festival club, having attended a separate opening as a member of the judging panel for the Irish Life awards.

The preview of *Hanging Around* that was due to be held on the same night was cancelled. To complete the Shakespearean comedy of errors, a sub-editor pulled up the computer template, set up in advance, from the following night's paper. This template carried the name of a separate innocent and unfortunate review, the one scheduled to cover *The Comeback* when it was due to open.

Act Two. A beautiful morning in the north Kildare countryside. I was admiring the neighbouring field where the straw had all been parcelled in big hair-curlers and carted off to straw-Valhalla when the telephone rang. The producer of the Pat Kenny radio programme broke the news. 'Do you know you have a review of a play that didn't take place in the paper this morning?' I was given twenty minutes to investigate what happened and did a telephone link, while the jubilant performers of *The Comeback*, due to make a comeback the following night, chuckled at the other end and Pat Kenny resonated on the sheer incompetence of it all.

I did the best I could, humouring the situation with stories of great disasters that had happened to other newspapers: like the London critic who arrived in with his review and was sacked because the theatre had burned down the night before. I also thought of suggesting that the reviewer should have taken over as racing tipster or we should have run the review in the astrology column, but I didn't get to say that on air, which is probably just as well.

Act Three. Years later, and the scene has changed. The reviewer who caused me such angst has gone on to a highly efficient and competent career in arts administration, her anonymity preserved. Different versions of the story have been touted in various media around the world. Sadly, the *Irish Press* itself is unlikely ever to make a comeback. Maybe I'll write a play about it myself for the theatre festival some day. You might call it 'theatre of the absurd'.

# STAN COSGROVE

*The Last shall be First!*

'When you hear the plaudits of triumph, let there sound in your ears the laughter you provoked by your failures', Monsignor Escriva wrote in *The Way*. Never have truer words been written — and their truth has been borne home to me more than once over the years.

A case in point was when I was invited to lunch at Kildangan in County Kildare some years ago by the late Roderick More O'Ferrall. I still flush with embarrassment even at the thought of the outcome of that inglorious day.

Among the distinguished attendance at this select luncheon was a lady who seized the moment and persuaded another guest to consider buying a hunter she had for sale. After the excellent meal, the steed was promptly presented outside the door.

I being the only qualified veterinarian among the assembly, I was readily prevailed upon to examine the beast. Rather than merely listen to the soundness of his wind and carry out the other customary physical checks from *terra firma*, I decided to go one better. The best way to test the beast, I declared dramatically, was to ride him myself (in the meantime impressing all present with my equestrian prowess).

Sporting a top-of-the-range thick tweed suit, I duly mounted with alacrity and galloped down into an adjoining field where everyone present could have a clear view of my riding display. I soon approached what I thought was a ditch along the top of the paddock, a shallow recess filled with running water. This, thought I, was the ideal opportunity to show the assembled onlookers what I was truly made of — by jumping the approaching obstacle in full flight. As luck would have it, the beast beneath me had other ideas. He promptly balked, pitching me over his neck right into the ditch. It was only then that I realised the obstacle in question was no ordinary ditch, but the overflow from a nearby septic tank!

There was never a more sorrowful sight (or smell!) than yours truly in his soiled tweeds, now on Shanks's mare and vainly pursuing the runaway. Worse, the stench was so bad that I had to head straight for my car and depart with the laughter of all Kildangan ringing in my ears. Afterwards, indeed, my unfortunate suit had to be sent twice to the cleaners before it could be seen out in company again.

Then there were the Mad Hatters races at the Phoenix Park and Leopardstown.

Notwithstanding such minor setbacks as the above, I always had an ambition to ride in a genuine horse race. Now this was not all that far fetched, I felt, as I used to ride out regularly with Mick Hurley's string on the Curragh at the time. As things transpired, however, the phrase 'anything but a jockey and far from a gentleman' might have served me better.

I made great preparations and redoubled my riding efforts before my racing début. The pre-race instructions from my trainer could not have been more confident. 'These are a lot of amateurs and they'll set off like hell,' he told me in the parade ring. 'Just sit tight and wait for them to come back to you.'

I did, but they didn't — starting at the rear, remaining there throughout, and finishing a bad last.

The taunts that greeted me on my way back to the jockeys' room were choice — 'Why didn't you wear rear lights?' 'You should have been arrested for loitering!' 'You missed the last bus!' And worse . . .

Yes, you've guessed it. I finished tailed off at Leopardstown too.

# EAMON CREGAN

It was in the early eighties, 1981 to be precise. This was the time when governments rose and fell like sports personalities; one minute you were riding high, the next you were flat on your back. Oh the fickleness of sports writers!

Anyway, to get on with my sceal, the FFers had a general election coming up in May/June. Limerick East was the venue and all the big guns were there: Des O'Malley, Peadar Clohessy, Michael Noonan, Jim Kemmy, Willie O'Dea, etc. Fianna Fáil would win two seats, but it was the third they wanted. But Michael Noonan and Jim Kemmy had things to say about that.

Kemmy had a strong city base and Noonan was the rising star for Fine Gael.

Then I realised how stupid a person can be, or was it ego?

I got a telephone call from a guy called Wall (no, nothing to do with the Walls of Limerick) at 12.40 p.m. on Tuesday. Would you stand for Fianna Fáil? Need to know by 1 p.m. Imagine Fianna Fáil headquarters ringing me about this. I know I had been asked some time before and refused, but I suppose ego is a terrible thing if it runs rampant. No one to discuss this with except Ann. I did not know where Des O'Malley was. In a panic, I got a mad rush of blood to the head and said yes by telephone. Ann naturally thought I was mad and sure I was.

I suppose you could guess what Des thought. Anyway, the die was cast. What next? Friends rallied round: Frank O'Sullivan, Noel, Conor, Sean Raleigh, Tom McInerney, Noreen, Tony, Therese, and many, many more.

HQ was in my office in O'Connell Street, maps of the city and the east plastered on the wall. Blindly, I started. My auctioneering business was handled by Ann Broderick from Athea (she has since died tragically in Australia) and we started canvassing. I was going to sweep all before me for

Fianna Fáil. They would get their third seat, but it wouldn't be me — either O'Dea or Clohessy.

After ten days it was announced that the 'Big Chief' was coming. Haughey was coming on a 'grand tour'. This was going to upset our schedule. We had people to see and hands to shake; this was disruption.

The Eagle landed in Sarsfield Barracks and came out to meet the plebs. I was knocked down in the rush to shake the great man's hand; O'Malley shuffled over, a limp handshake; O'Dea, a big O'Dealing smile on his face; Peadar, half-shy.

I was about to meet the leader of Fianna Fáil; I had taken three weeks off work, did no training with Limerick even though we were meeting Tipp in Thurles; spent whatever bit of money I had just to help get the third seat; and here he was, 'Our Leader'.

Being the last to shake his hand (I suppose he was tired) I took his hand and shook it. Very limp. I did not realise I was that tall. He looked at me for about two seconds and turned away to start his cavalcade through Limerick.

It suddenly dawned on me on that sunny day in Sarsfield Barracks, that this man had not a clue who I was. The embarrassment was all over my face, but he did not see it because he was gone.

I decided there and then that never ever would I put myself in that position again.

# PADDY CULLEN

*An Incident of '78*

The story. I never thought in all the times I played in Croke Park that the Canal end held so many people. Now creeping towards its twentieth anniversary, I am still approached by people who said that they were there — they saw what happened.

It was a good run for the footballers of Dublin. We were

playing in our fourth All-Ireland final and going for three in a row that fateful September of '78.

History tells us who the 'enemy' was — Kerry. History tells us who the hero was — that Fred Astaire of Kerry football, Mikey Sheehy. But who was the villain? There are mixed views.

I ran from my goalkeeping position to collect a harmless dropping ball falling towards the Hogan stand. As I collected the ball and delivered it over the incoming Ger Power's head, both Ger and I crushed shoulders. The referee, Seamus Aldridge (the villain?), blew his whistle and awarded a free kick to me (the villain?); but lo and behold, it was not to me at all. (Panic!)

As all good eccentric goalkeepers would do, I queried his decision. (Fool!)

Meanwhile, Mikey Sheehy was placing the ball hurriedly. I started running back to my goal, but Mikey had chipped the ball into my net, as I wrapped myself around the goalpost. Most embarrassing! That man of script, Con Houlihan, wrote: 'Paddy ran like a woman who realised she left a cake burning in the oven.'

The aftermath. The embarrassment only started in the ensuing weeks and months. Letters from America: 'What the hell were you doing?' putting it mildly! TV transmissions in Australia, Europe and Britain didn't lie either — more letters to open!

Postscript. Is Seamus Aldridge contributing to this book? Will this be the end of all the discussions? You've seen the film; now read the book. What a scoop for Seán Power!

# BRIAN D'ARCY

It was always an adage in journalism that what people wished to tell you should be an advertisement. What people want to hide is news.

A most embarrassing moment is news, and if I had

any sense I wouldn't tell you.

I'm long enough on the road now to know that there's no such thing as having a most embarrassing moment. Throughout life I've had a series of very embarrassing moments and, at the time, each of them was most embarrassing.

I can think of the time I visited a famous hotel in Waterville in County Kerry. I was mightily impressed with the grandeur and the magnificence of the scenery. Before entering the dining-room, I visited the men's room. There, amid many Americans, was a man dressed in a green blazer. We spoke haltingly and in a reserved fashion, as strangers ought to do in the men's toilet.

It was obvious he was an American. His dress, his blazer and his accent betrayed him. We spoke about Ireland, about the beauty of Kerry and about the friendliness of the Irish.

Wanting to prove the point, I shook his hand and welcomed him to Ireland, to Waterville and to this magnificent hotel. 'I hope you enjoy your stay here', I told him, full of enthusiasm and fáilte.

Feeling a satisfied citizen, I made for the dining-room. The person who was with me then proceeded to introduce me to the owner of the hotel, a Mr Mulcahy, who was on holidays from America. And yes, you're right, it was the very same man whom, two minutes earlier, I had welcomed to Ireland in the toilet of his own hotel.

The embarrassment of an insignificant stranger in Kerry welcoming the millionaire owner to his own hotel still makes me blush today.

Or, there was the time when I was with the Jimmy Magee All-Stars in Las Vegas. I'm not a sun worshipper. But in Las Vegas there was a beautiful pool in the hotel. So, with all the fervour of a sun-seeking Irishman, I put on my togs and went down to take a swim in the outdoor pool.

At the side of the pool there was a very bronzed, heavy, well-built, athletic Texan. He was snuggling as close as anyone could to an equally bronzed, well-shaped and leggy,

American model type. I tiptoed past them. I didn't want to disturb their obvious peace. As I went by him, he snapped his head back, took the name of my ultimate boss in vain, looked at my sickeningly pale skin, compared it to his own bronzed artifice, and shouted at the top of his voice for all to hear, 'Jees, the last time I saw anything that white, it was dead.'

But, undoubtedly, my most embarrassing moment was the day I got drunk saying Mass in Lourdes.

I had been invited by the late Cardinal O'Fiaich to Lourdes. It was my first time there. And, as part of the normal celebrations, there is a huge international Mass on a Wednesday afternoon in the underground basilica.

Every pilgrim in Lourdes on that day tries to attend. The underground basilica can seat in excess of 25,000 people. Usually every priest who is there concelebrates Mass. On the day I was there, in excess of 200 priests were concelebrating.

Cardinal O'Fiaich was the main celebrant. Because I was with his party, I was the last priest to receive from the chalice.

There was a French Dominican who was master of ceremonies on that day. He picked up a jug of 'water' and put a drop into each of the twenty or so chalices on the altar, to purify them.

He adroitly emptied the contents out of each chalice into one remaining chalice, which he handed to me to drink. Not knowing French and not knowing any better, I did. I drank an absolutely full chalice of water in about six gulps. Except that it wasn't water. Contrary to the usual custom, he in fact purified the chalices with wine.

As the world and its wife knows, I'm a pioneer. And as soon as the wine hit me, it went to my head. My head started spinning. I knew I had a silly grin on my face. I held grimly on to the altar, knowing that if I moved hand or foot I'd end up in a heap on the floor. I remained there grinning foolishly at everyone who looked in my direction. And there were many who did.

Cardinal O'Fiaich must have recognised what had happened. He said the blessing, with me still gripping resolutely to the end of the altar and still smiling inanely into his face. I was paralysed with fear. I knew I was drunk, and I knew that one wrong move and everyone else would know I was drunk too.

The Cardinal wisely sent a friend out to link me in. I was then linked up to my hotel room, put on the bed where I slept for two hours and woke up with the greatest hangover I've ever had in my life — actually, the only hangover I've ever had.

It put the longing for drink off me. I was sick, I was sore, I was embarrassed. After all, only in Lourdes could a pioneer get drunk saying Mass.

No disrespect was meant and no disrespect was taken. But on this occasion at least, all those jokes about the power of Lourdes water came home to roost.

# ANTHONY DALY

I have had many an embarrassing moment during the years I've spent hurling, but I don't think any stand out as being the worst. Funnily enough, the most embarrassing moment I can recall was actually during a soccer match. Before I joined the county panel a few years back, I used to play soccer for a local Ennis club which played in the premier division of the Clare League.

All concerned took the game very seriously, and we enjoyed quite a bit of success over a two to three-year period. Our manager at the time was a very vocal character and regularly got into trouble with referees. On this particular Sunday we were playing in a cup final that was the showpiece of Clare Junior soccer. Played at the seaside town of Lahinch, it was a very exciting game and finished two-all, after extra time.

During the course of the game, our manager had become involved verbally with the referee and was ordered to remove himself from the grounds. He did so, and was sitting on the boundary wall, where we could still hear his shrill voice distinctly. It was ordered that the result should be decided by the dreaded penalty kick shoot-out.

All the crowd gathered around the goal where the kicks were to be taken, and we went to the wall to get our instructions as to what order to kick in. The manager named the five and yours truly was to be first up. The last advice he gave us was, 'Whatever you do, don't miss.'

I approached the goal with the ball and placed it on the spot. The crowd hushed as I ran up and blasted the ball high and well over the crossbar. There was a deafening roar from the opposition supporters as I turned to make the lonely walk back to the centre.

The roar turned to silence, as I walked back mortified. But then came the crowning moment. From the corner of the boundary wall came the response from our infamous manager: 'You nearly hit a seagull', at which the crowd erupted again, this time into laugher at the comment. I nearly died of embarrassment, and to make matters worse, we lost by just the one kick — mine.

# RONNIE DELANEY

*Have Gun, Will Travel*

If you are thinking of stealing a few yards on the opposition, then be forewarned.

I was a bit nonplussed to be invited again by Seán Power to contribute 'an embarrassing moment' for his latest book in aid of the Children's Cancer Fund. Embarrassing moments are something you want to forget, not recall for all to read. Like the time I was a little bit previous and arrived a week early one cold February evening in Ballina for the Mayo Sports Stars banquet in the Downhill Hotel. This is all the more absurd when you consider how late functions usually start in Mayo.

But I can recall one of the most embarrassing moments of all time in sport. You see, I had the incredible experience of witnessing the only false start ever in an Olympic marathon race. Conveniently for me it was some forty years ago at the Melbourne Olympiad. It was 1 December 1956 and the official starter carefully brought the entire marathon field of runners under starter's orders before the largest crowd in Olympic history. He sensationally adjudged that a Swedish competitor, Evert Nyberg, had broken, immediately firing the gun a second time to signal a false start, and recalled all and sundry to the starting line again.

It was undoubtedly 'the best laugh of the 1956 Olympic Games' wrote Dave Guiney, the distinguished Olympic historian. But such was the fair-play ethic in the olden days that not even a one-inch advantage would be tolerated, even in a race measuring 26 miles 385 yards.

If it is of any interest or relevance to this story, I am admirably qualified to act as a race starter. I am probably one of the few Irish men who knows how to say, 'On your marks, get set and bang' in at least ten different languages, not including erse. This was essential knowledge when I was a competitor if one was not to be left standing at the start of many a race on foreign fields, or in arenas, to be precise. The most recent time I started a race was at the Penn Relays in Philadelphia, one of the legendary sporting carnivals in the US, where successive Irish athletes over the years have thrilled the crowded spectators by running victoriously in the colours of Villanova, Arkansas and Providence College.

News of the one occasion I was involved in a somewhat embarrassing and potentially disastrous start of a race must have since filtered through to editor Seán Power. Let me try and recall it.

It was a St Stephen's Day 10 K road race in Dublin some twenty years ago, sponsored by my club Crusaders AC. A former adversary of mine and clubmate, Jimmy O'Neill, was helping me with the start just outside the RDS on Simmonscourt Road. The over eager competitors, hundreds of them, were jostling each other as they came into line. Jimmy was about to pass me the loaded starter's pistol when it suddenly, not to mention prematurely, went off with a bang. As far as the runners were concerned the race was on. They took off *en masse*, trampling the less fortunate Jimmy into the ground. Happily, he suffered no more serious damage than superficial gunpowder burns, scratched knees and a much-damaged pride.

You can now see that starting a race can be somewhat perilous, certainly embarrassing, and requires a degree of courage and, above all, the athletic agility I demonstrated on St Stephen's Day in getting out of the way of that human stampede.

So on your marks, get set and — I warn you — don't break before I fire the gun.

# PROINSIAS DE ROSSA

*The Last Time I was Locked (Out)* or *Going to the Rails for Charlie*

Embarrassing moments are things we try to forget, particularly the ones that continue to make us cringe, until time soothes the hurt ego.

There is one such moment which I can smile about now, just about.

It was fourteen years ago, 9 March 1982 to be exact. I had been elected to the Dáil for the first time. I was as proud as punch. No one had given me a chance, not even my own party. Now I was one of the three Workers Party TDs whose votes Fianna Fáil needed desperately. So it was sweet revenge to be there at all, and great satisfaction for the small number of activists who had worked so tirelessly for ten years before in Finglas and Ballymun.

Within hours I had gone from complete anonymity outside of my constituency, to having the national media hanging on my every word, mostly multiples of the same words, in themselves a source of perennial embarrassment.

To my surprise, having for a long time avoided radio and TV because of my stammer, I discovered it didn't matter to anyone but me, which did wonders for my self-confidence and my sense of self-importance.

So, following weeks of discussion with Fianna Fáil as to what we could expect of them if we voted for them as a minority government, the three of us were in the Dáil chamber waiting to vote for C. J. Haughey. Suddenly Paddy Gallagher needed a smoke. While we knew virtually nothing about Dáil procedures, we did know that the vote would not happen for about eight minutes.

The three of us moved out on to the landing at the entrance to the chamber. We were met by this wall of Fianna Fáil supporters. They shook our hands and slapped our backs; some even whispered that they were really socialists. After what seemed like only seconds, we turned to go back inside to vote when, to our horror, we found we were locked out.

Oh, Christ! I thought, another general election. How could we have done something so incredibly stupid!

Joe Sherlock shouted to follow him, as he pushed his way through the crowd towards a door on the right. Going through, we found ourselves in a narrow corridor. Halfway down, there was another doorway to the left. Rushing through that door, we arrived among a gaggle of startled journalists looking down into the Dáil chamber. We moved quickly to the right, stepped over a waist-high rail and found ourselves in the Tá lobby. We were ushered like sheep through the gate to be counted. There would be no general election after all.

I am not sure how the other two felt, but I was mortified. It was bad enough to have to vote for Fianna Fáil at all, but to have had to go to such lengths to do it was undignified and embarrassing beyond belief.

The media, and particularly the cartoonists, had a field day — depicting us jumping from the balcony and falling on our heads on the floor below. I have had many other embarrassing moments, both before and since, but none has been accompanied by such public humiliation — so far!

# BRYAN DOBSON

As you can imagine, anyone who appears regularly on television will carry with them the unhappy memory of many embarrassing moments. It is one of the occupational hazards of live broadcasting. My considerate colleagues in the RTE newsroom still like to remind me of the occasion on which I informed the nation that, on the eve of an important soccer international, the injured Niall Quinn was being treated by the team psychotherapist. This was also the night on which I promoted Dick Spring to Taoiseach, which caused great amusement but, who knows, may yet be prophetic.

In a radio interview about horses — about which I know nothing — my interviewee, who was telling me about half-bred horses, was stunned when I asked him to explain the difference between half breeds and whole breeds. I still cringe when I recall a short and ill-prepared interview I did on 'Morning Ireland' with Mary Holland about the talks between John Hume and Gerry Adams which led to the ceasefire, in which I asked her to explain to me what was in this process for the SDLP. 'Peace, of course', she replied. How do you follow that up?

The lesson from these, and more I will not mention, is always, be prepared and concentrate on the job. But despite my own advice, I can still guarantee that in a year from now I will have yet more embarrassments to add to my mental archive.

# KEN DOHERTY

My most embarrassing moment happened when I was 10 years of age.

My brother and I went away for a weekend to Baltinglass, Co. Wicklow, to visit my aunt, uncle and two cousins.

My cousin suggested that we go down to the farm and play. One of my cousins climbed up on to a wall and threw down a 10p and said if I wanted it I had to go and get it. What I did not know was that he had thrown it into the slurry pit. I stepped into the pit and ended up neck deep in pig manure.

My uncle had to come and rescue me and carried me through the town back to our house on his bike. I ended up being bathed in disinfectant, and it is only in the last two months that the smell has gone.

# JOHN DRENNAN

Writing about the most embarrassing moment of your life is a difficult task. Life in general appears to consist of a series of blunders from which we learn absolutely nothing. Just as well. There would be no craic at all if you weren't making a bit of a gobshite of yourself every now and again.

For the average Irish man most of our embarrassing moments are centred around the subject of women. However, as this is a clean book, we will keep that out of it.

Apart from women, drink is the chief culprit of any litany of shame, so we'll stick to that.

There is a tradition in Maynooth College that in a particular square after dining many of the clerical professors wander sedately digesting fine wines and six-course dinners. It's a fine square, with many exotic trees, about which more later.

The equanimity of such strolls was disturbed only once prior to this story when, after the laicisation of Maynooth, some female students decided to sunbathe in the square, leading to much unhappiness amongst the Ghengis Khan wing of the professorial strollers. This was dealt with quickly and efficiently and the grass of Joe's Square has ever since been safe from the flesh of sunbathing women.

My story begins in a local pub when one morning, in my youthful innocence, I decided to see how much whiskey I could consume before falling down. I think perhaps I had been watching too many of those cowboy movies where the hero walks in, snaps up his whiskey, downs it in one gulp, slaps his glass on the counter and walks off unaffected after twenty. This was not the case with me, and soon a fatherly barman was putting his hand on my shoulder saying, 'Ah will you go home now, son.'

Life would have been much simpler if I had, but then we never do.

Instead, I developed a strange passionate desire to attend a lecture on medieval English in a hall right beside the square. Unfortunately I never quite made it. The discovery of a shopping trolley in the hall beside the lecture theatre promised much more entertainment, and soon the students inside were treated to a mix of wahoos and curses, the latter following loud crashes as the trolley regularly slammed into the wall.

After a while I tired of this and climbed up the stairs, determined to make a statement on the nature of medieval English. This, I am reliably told, consisted of f—k Chaucer and f—k medieval English you boring old bat. The lecturer, a remarkably equable woman, merely murmured, 'I see rag week has come early this year.' I was not in a position to hear this as I had fallen down the stairs.

The nadir was yet to come.

Having left, it was my misfortune to then fall into the most remarkably complicated bush/tree in which I have ever found myself. Escape was impossible. After ten minutes I abandoned myself to wails and curses.

Moments later, in what was my second last lucid moment, I looked up to see four elderly clerical gentlemen from the classics department looking in curiously, all of whom knew me as I was intermittently doing the subject. They rapidly disappeared in the direction of security.

My last lucid memory is, ten minutes later, being lifted out of the tree by two security guards who drove me gently away murmuring, 'Ah will you go home now.'

This time, I did, safe in the knowledge that if I got away with this I could get away with anything. I did. Some would say I have continued to get away with anything since.

# JOE DUFFY

*Tears for Souvenirs*

I tried to kick the stolen purse under the seat in front of me on the bus, but it refused to budge. Just as in my worst nightmare my foot kept missing the purse, like a swinging pendulum in a grandfather clock.

I couldn't kick the purse, but I was kicking myself! Why had I stolen the purse? How was I going to get rid of it, now that the man who owned it was standing at the front of the bus, demanding its return — knowing as he did, that someone on the bus had the purse.

I was trapped. I was embarrassed, ashamed and panicking.

I could still see the zipped grey purse on the floor — I could see little else. Who else could see it? All I could think of, in my panic when the shopkeeper jumped on to the coach just as it was about to depart, screaming in German for his precious purse, was how to get rid of it without anyone knowing.

I squeezed it out of my pocket and dropped it on to the floor. I now realised that once the owner of the purse, accompanied by our schoolteacher, marched down the centre aisle of the coach searching everybody for the stolen item, the purse would be found.

And I would be exposed for what I was, a thief, a robber, the culprit who had let the school down in a foreign country. Worse still, I wasn't even sitting beside my buddy who might share the blame with me.

I could either own up or simply let the purse be found and hope someone else would get the blame. 'Miss, I never saw that purse. Somebody must have thrown it on the floor and kicked it back to our seat.'

What had possessed me to rob it from the shop anyway? So I didn't have much money. Everyone else was buying souvenirs for their mothers; but they didn't have much money either.

In the mêlée, as straining hands reached out to pay for the stupid snow-filled Tyrolean souvenirs, I saw the owner turn his back, and in a moment my straining hand was in my pocket. The purse was stolen.

I hadn't planned it. Honest. It wasn't premeditated — if it had been a killing, I would have got off on a plea of manslaughter — 'I did it on the spur of the moment, your honour!'

But how was I going to get out of this awful embarrassment?

The shopkeeper was advancing. The teacher marched along beside him, as if she were escorting a visiting dignitary around a welcoming guard of honour.

I sweated. I prayed. Tears welled up.

Without thinking, I reached down and grabbed the purse. I jumped up, waving it over my head. 'I have it', I shouted, as if the strength of my voice would somehow drown my fear.

As the red-faced, angry shopkeeper grabbed his purse back, I muttered something about believing that I had paid for it. Thankfully, his German expletives were beyond our knowledge of the language.

I plumped back into the seat as the silence enveloped the bus. The teacher slouched back to her front seat, quietly embarrassed.

I pushed my button nose up against the window, the heat of my red face melting into the condensation.

A tap on my shoulder. I looked around, tears in my eyes, as my classmate spat at me, 'Are you bleeding mad or what? Why didn't you kick it under the seat?'

# BISHOP JOSEPH DUFFY

### *In Somebody else's House*

My aunt and uncle lived in a sedate part of the country, well away from the troubled border area where our family lived. They had one son, some years younger than me, the apple of their eye. Because they had a big house and were both very generous by nature, there was an endless queue of teenage nephews and nieces every summer, eager to sample a higher standard of living than was our lot at home. There was, for example, a grass tennis court, and lashings of raspberries and strawberries from the garden every day for dessert after lunch. Being young and taking it for granted that our elders were there for our benefit, we made the most of the hospitality, without much thought of repayment in kind or in anything else.

On occasion, however, there was a modest response of conscience, like helping to wash the dishes or weed the flower beds. It was also a house where one respected the furniture and was careful not to soil the carpets. In fact, carpets were a prolonged topic of conversation during one particular summer holiday I spent there. There were several visits to expensive warehouses in Dublin and exhaustive discussions with other aunts and uncles and more local authorities on the subject. If possible, one tried discreetly to avoid these exchanges, but it soon became the major theme of discourse at breakfast, dinner and tea. Finally, one day, the deal was done and a beautiful Axminster carpet was expertly and securely fitted on the drawing-room floor.

The matter of the carpet should have ended there. After all, once you have seen a new carpet and admired it, there is nothing more to be said. As well as that, the sudden arrival of cousins from another part of the country made for more interesting times. There was tennis at the house and swimming at the lake a few miles out the road. The neighbouring farmers were busy at the hay and were glad of the little help we were happy to give. The loan of a few bicycles made getting around easy and independent. There may have been the occasional rainy day, but one remembers more the long hours of brilliant sunshine with not a single cloud in the sky.

Except for one wet day when we had to spend the whole morning in the house. My usual escape on this kind of day was to get my hands on a book and disappear out of sight. This particular day turned out a little differently. At lunchtime my aunt suggested that, if I found the afternoon long on my hands, I might hoover the new carpet. In my own time, she said, and only if I felt like it. She then went off with the others in the car to do her shopping and to show them the town. I was quite pleased to be left on my own with only an unhoovered carpet between me and the rest of my book. The first job was to find the hoover. I should explain that while I had often seen the thing in action, it had always been at a respectable distance. There was, however, no problem. My aunt had said that it was kept in the utility room off the kitchen. And sure enough, there it was, ready for use. In fact there were two of them. I took out the newer-looking one, complete with bag, and in no time at all got it plugged in and moving. It began smoothly enough, but very soon became jerky and then stopped of its own accord. The reason was alarming. The hoover was sinking into the thick pile of carpet instead of merely taking the loose hairs and dust off the surface. Then I spotted two deep green tracks on either side of the machine. This, I knew, was real trouble. I pulled out the plug and removed the cover of the motor. To my horror what I was looking at were the unmistakable blades of a lawn mower caught in wedges of tangled wool and tiny tufts of green grass turning yellow. The shock to the system was total. I was glued to the floor in a state of dumb terror.

Worse was to follow. Before I could move or gather my wits about me, I heard the footsteps of my uncle in the front hallway. He had arrived home, much earlier than usual, for his tea. As if he knew where I was, he came to the door of the room and called out my name in his usual cheerful tone of voice. I was too confused to reply. But in my misery, it occurred to me that this was the ultimate disaster. I was caught in the act, aching in every joint with guilt and despair. There was nowhere to run away and hide, nowhere to bury the evidence of destruction. I remember to this day the puzzled eyes of my uncle turning slowly from the panic on my face to the ruins on the floor. He then paused, stroked his chin, and quietly reassured me that we need not say what happened. A most embarrassing moment had passed.

# SEAN DUIGNAN

*'You Let Me Down!'*

A disturbingly large percentage of my most embarrassing moments have been linked to my pal Mike Burns. They always consist of me making a show of myself and Mike shaking his head reprovingly while bailing me out. This incident in New York some time in 1968 is typical. I had just discovered the great American invention, the dry Martini, and Manhattan was going round and round. We were in a well-known Irish bar not far from the United Nations. A group was playing 'Come Back to Erin' stuff on a small bandstand. Mike went off to the toilet and never came back.

Some time later, the MC announced: 'Ladies and gentlemen, we are privileged to have one of Ireland's greatest entertainers in our company. I think if we give him a round of applause, he may be persuaded to give us a song. Ladies and gentlemen, Sean Duignan.' Too late, it dawned on me why Mike had been so long away from his bar stool.

To make a long story short, I allowed myself to be led to my execution. I actually thought I wasn't all that bad, given the short notice on top of the Martinis. I blame the bar combo who I swear to my dying day kept playing 'I'll Take You Home Again, Kathleen', when I was trying to sing 'Here's a Toast to You, Claddagh'.

Unfortunately, however, unrefined elements among the bar clientele were bereft of cultural appreciation. I clearly remember some oaf shouting, 'Throw the bum out.' And then, to my absolute astonishment, I was rudely interrupted, politely but firmly led from the bandstand to the door, and unceremoniously deposited on the sidewalks of New York.

The worst part was that at least another fifteen minutes passed while I waited outside the bar, torn between indignation and mortification, for Mike to come out. I was practically dancing with fury by the time he eventually emerged. I had just started to splutter my outrage when he stopped me with a wave of his hand, fixed me with a deeply wounded stare, and then pronounced judgment: 'You let me down!'

# DERMOT EARLEY

*'Say Cheese.'*

Knocking the ball out of my goalkeeper's hands into our own net, and remarking, 'You must be the ambassador's daughter', when in fact she was (is) his wife, are two mildly traumatic incidents that come to mind. However, a most embarrassing moment in my life occurred at Dublin Airport quite some years ago.

My sister, her husband and family were returning to Australia after an exciting holiday in Ireland. There must have been thirty of the extended family including the departees in the departure area. The airport seemed particularly busy and it was difficult to keep track of everyone, especially children, as people checked in, moved luggage along the queue and bade their farewells. I don't usually bring my camera — always forget it for special events — but this day I took it with me and had two exposures left on a roll that had probably been opened a year earlier. I would record this special occasion.

My suggestion for a shot of everyone was greeted with enthusiasm. The difficulty was how to get everyone together and where to take the picture. On my instructions a few of the adults formed a line. My task now was to get everyone else into the frame. As the group got bigger people began to notice. Two businessmen rushing for a connection were not amused when they had to detour around this bunch in the middle of the departure lounge. Most others were taken in by the distraction and just watched. An American lady close by exclaimed, 'How wonderful!' when she understood what was happening. This prompted my mother to get into deep conversation with her, explain the momentous event and give her our family history. As mother was eased back into the picture a few of the children had broken free from the ranks.

The courteous Aer Lingus staff and the alert airport

security personnel had now seen the problem and came to my aid. Let's help out, get this over quickly and have normal airport activities restored as soon as possible, was their goal. They stopped everything — check-in, conveyor belts and movement. In a few seconds all was ready for the picture. The attention of the moving world in this neck of the woods was upon us.

I focused quickly, looked up, and was about to utter the immortal, 'Say cheese', when my brother Paul, about 12 at the time, bolted from the front towards me. I ate him silently through clenched teeth and had him back in line in seconds. I checked the focus again, but Paul bolted once more with something to say. Before he knew it I had him by the back of the arm, pinching hard and guiding him into place, informing him what would happen when we got home. When he attempted to come towards me a third time to say something, he saw my anger, shrugged his shoulders and said, 'OK.' I was in position quickly, called 'Cheese' and clicked the camera. Relief all around. 'Just one more, the last one', I declared, got everyone smiling and recorded the occasion again. 'Thank you', I said out loud, and a gentle ripple of applause greeted the break-up of the group.

People then turned away focusing their attention back to what they were doing before they were interrupted, and in the momentary silence that occurs when attention is diverted, brother Paul, who was now by my side, uttered loudly, clearly and unforgettably, 'I thought you were supposed to take the cover off the lens.' The words hung in the air, appeared to vibrate off the roof, walls and luggage, and as I slowly turned the covered lens towards me, there erupted guffaws of laughter from everyone around me. 'I was trying to tell you, but you wouldn't heed me,' said Paul, adding to the embarrassment.

I have never taken a photograph or stood in for one since without remembering the lens incident or without experiencing a small rise of the glow of embarrassment.

# DESMOND EGAN

*'My heart in hiding . . .' (Gerard Manley Hopkins)*

Was it my playing in the under-12 violin competition at Sligo Feis Ceoil when a string went in the cursed bow and drifted forlornly after every nervy note? Worse was to follow: the absolute dissonance of that last, double-stopped chord on which my performance (for want of a better word) finished. Ugh! I can hear it right this very second: the sheer awfulness of it, the music murder, the *coup de grâce* to the composer's dream! On stage, too! It will all go with me to the grave.

Or maybe that terrible moment — should I pick it? — when, at my first dance (in the Royal Hotel) I had finally churned my emotions into enough control to ask the lovely Anne for a dance — only to be turned down with a snigger. Death, where is thy sting?

Or the day I volunteered during religion class at boarding school (where everything had double the intensity) that the letters I.N.R.I. at the base of the crucifix stood for 'Iron nails rivetted in'? Part of received wisdom at the Dean Kelly School, Athlone. The horror of having provoked both class and teacher — the formidable Fr John Lynch — to join unexpectedly together in a sudden avalanche of laughter at yours truly! And I such a goody-good.

Or perhaps that more recent, more subtle savaging when, as important juror at the hosting of Corcomroe poetry competition, I was haranguing a large audience from the top of the mound where (it seems) the old bardic school met; and a non-involved local, who happened to drive by in his Prefect, wound down the window and let out a huge Clare yahoo at the lot of us? Parting shot indeed: even still I squirm at the thought of our pretentiousness and that epiphany of attitudes and of worlds.

But no: killing though all those experiences were — and

62

to be embarrassed is to die a little — I think they must yield to another. The worst. The pits.

I had been asked by a second cousin to sing a song at his wedding reception. Believe it or not, such things sometimes happened: I had the reputation in those days of being a singer and had not destroyed it by involvement in various operas, in one of which — *Maritana* — the great Louis Browne made his début. This meant, in practice, that I might occasionally sing in the next room for visitors to our house. Or not at all. Because in those days I was abominably shy, searingly, self-destructively so. Shy and a dreamer: a horrible combination. So shy, in fact, that I would panic even on going into a room full of strangers, shaken by the challenge of all that otherness; and could be counted on to remain tongue tied and silent for the duration. What a disability for a teenager! How many times did I sweat blood behind my simpering agreements and exaggerated interest in nothing much. To the point eventually, that I would sometimes force myself to go in among people just as an exercise, a discipline, an attempt at self-mastery, knowing that shyness is a kind of pride, a convoluted arrogance. I remember pushing through the swing doors into the Palace Bar one afternoon, and into the astonished gaze of poor old Polecat Shine and his audience, with something approaching the resolution which a cowboy hero would muster heading into the saloon where the crooks are hiding, hands over his trusty six-guns for the final shoot-out. What awaited me, I well knew: terror, confusion on all sides, a shotgun blast of self-consciousness and that cursed reddening of the cheeks which always gave the game away.

But back to the wedding. It struck me, when asked to sing, that the impact of any singing would be greater by far if there were someone there to accompany the performers — I wrongly assumed there would be more than one. Probably my shyness had something to do with this too. (Or was it just my natural tendency to shoot myself in the foot — an inclination which, my friends are kind enough to remind me, I have never lost. Thanks again, Jack.) So, weeks before, I had made my suggestion. Good idea. No problem. Glad you mentioned it.

Came the big day. I sat at the wedding breakfast, already a bag of nerves, hardly able to eat — at the thought of facing this large, important group of relations and friends, and at such close quarters. Much easier from a stage, in a darkened hall. Thump, thump, thump.

The iron ritual of an Irish wedding reception had been observed to the letter. The best man — 'a great speaker' — had whispered and nerved through his fumble of words. The telegrams had been read — including ones about their only troubles being little ones, and the patter of tiny feet. The mother of the bride had been thanked, fulsomely; and the father, as an afterthought. Welcome offered into the other family as if it had enormous significance. To the bride and groom! A few witty words from the priest . . . Then my turn had come. Applause, after an over-generous introduction.

I stood up in the sudden quiet and looked around for the accompanist. Accompanist? Oh, the accompanist! I knew I'd forget something. Anyone here play the piano? He needs an accompanist.

He needs an accompanist! The dreadful, stomach-churning phrase bounced and echoed round the reception room. The waiters looked up. Someone heading for the gents froze at the door.

Silence.

And slowly my poor over-used cheeks began to redden. The silence hardened like the icing on the wedding cake. The audience of eyes narrowed. I could almost hear people saying, 'The cheek!' Accompanist, how are you! Far from an accompanist he was reared. I wouldn't mind but his father hasn't a note in his head. I blame his parents . . . college boy!

And something, for the umpteenth time, something hyper delicate, quiveringly sensitive, something too fastidious for this harsh world gave a little kick, curled up inside me, and began to die. Oh even now, decades, worlds, miseries, disasters later, the memory spreads, takes over. The ultimate blush.

(Desmond Egan has published fifteen collections of poetry and one of prose. A full-time writer, he lives outside Newbridge. People think he has changed a lot over the years.)

# AENGUS FANNING

*My May Altar Ego*

I was 12, a first year pupil at the Christian Brothers secondary school in Tralee, a school beautifully located in the town park, where the lawns and flower beds were tended by Mr Greaney, an expert gardener, but a man of very few words and someone of whom we were all a little afraid.

One lovely afternoon in early May in the late 1950s, I cycled down Rock Street on my way back to school after lunch, conscious of being even later than usual. The anxiety which gripped me was heightened by the realisation that, as I pedalled up Denny Street, there was not a fellow pupil in sight. I knew that I was on my own, probably a full ten minutes later than even the latest straggler, and that the wrath of the elderly and still formidable Brother Turner was again about to descend on me.

At the entrance to the town park, about 400 yards from the school, stood the imposing cut stone building of the County Hall, the seat of local government in Kerry, where the immaculate gardens were also part of Mr Greaney's domain.

As I turned the corner on my green BSA bike, I was struck by what I was sure was real, even divine, inspiration.

Mr Greaney's flowers were flourishing splendidly, the brilliant colours of his tulips, lilies, forget-me-nots, primroses and wallflowers being at their best in the early summer sunshine. I thought of Brother Turner's rather wistful-looking May altar. I knew it was a disappointment to him and that he was embarrassed at the prospect of being a clear loser in the May altar contest, one of the areas where inter-brother rivalry was at its fiercest.

No sooner had the thought occurred to me than the deed followed. I laid my bicycle against a lamp standard, jumped over the railings of the County Hall, and within a few seconds (aware that Mr Greaney, if he was watching, could see the gardens from his house beside the school) had cut with my penknife and gathered a spectacular and generous bundle of flowers.

Minutes later, I was in the classroom, explaining my lateness to Brother Turner. I had told my mother that the May altar was in need of a bit of a lift and she had permitted me to bring as many flowers from her own garden as I could carry back to school after lunch, I lied.

'Good, very good, maith an bhuachaill', said Brother Turner who, when he was pleased, made what I can only describe as a low purring sound. Now he was purring louder than any of us had ever remembered before.

Lessons were halted, and the class was set to work cutting and trimming the flowers, filling vases and jam jars with water, and decorating the best May altar the school had ever seen, one that would completely overshadow those in the adjoining classrooms of Brother Phelan and Brother Farrell.

For the first time I was Brother Turner's blue-eyed boy. 'What can I do to thank your mother', he would say, interrupting his purring as he worked with a happy bunch of boys at the altar.

The euphoria was not, alas, to last. We had practically finished our labour of love when the door burst open and a furious Brother Doherty, the school superior, stormed in with Mr Greaney close up in his slipstream.

'Fanning, come out,' said Brother Doherty. 'You have stolen Mr Greaney's flowers, the property of the County

Council and the ratepayers of Kerry, and he saw you do it.'

Brother Turner looked shaken, and the rest of the class were enjoying the entertainment of rare quality as I stepped out into the corridor where Brother Doherty gave me twenty-one slaps of the dreaded black leather, ten on one hand and eleven on the other. I know because I counted every one of them.

Brother Doherty, with Mr Greaney at his side looking grimly satisfied, propelled me with a final shove back into the classroom, where I expected more punishment from Brother Turner.

To my surprise, Brother Turner seemed quite phlegmatic. He didn't actually pat me on the head, but he got on with the normal business of class, and I sensed that he was not entirely displeased.

The marvellous altar stayed in place all through a beautiful month of May. We prayed before it several times a day, and every so often some of us brought in a few extra flowers to keep it topped up, so to speak.

It was probably my earliest insight into the pragmatism of human nature. I realised that to have the best May altar in the school mattered more to Brother Turner than the anger of the superior and Mr Greaney and his embarrassment before them. In fact, he was not at all put out by the dubious provenance of the May altar flowers and he seemed to look on me with more favour than he ever had before, favour tempered with prudent caution lest he should be seen to actually condone what I had done.

Though Machiavelli was someone I didn't get around to reading for another few years, I began to realise that Brother Turner, at least on the question of May altars, firmly believed that the end justified the means.

Perhaps he should have been in politics, or law, or even both.

# BRIAN FARRELL

It was my first television appearance. RTE had been on the air about five weeks. A phone call from Peter (P. P.) O'Reilly, editor of the station's first television magazine programme, to appear in a discussion on 'Broadsheet' had turned into an invitation to chair the item.

I was delighted. What a wonderful chance on a brand new medium. Of course, there was no question of any training. The invitation came at lunchtime. By 5.30 that same evening I made my way to a still incomplete Montrose.

It looked like a building site. There were cement mixers and concrete blocks all over the place, in a sea of mud. No point in heading for the main door — it wasn't yet finished. Instead, I skirted the side of the building until I reached a side entrance and clambered upstairs.

I had never been inside a television studio before and my previous couple of years broadcasting from the old sound radio studios in the GPO building in Henry Street offered few clues. Nor was I experienced as a viewer; we had only bought a television set that Christmas, just before RTE television went on air. Everything was strange, novel and a little intimidating.

The studio was small. Thanks to some very inventive direction the 'Broadsheet' team created the illusion of a large open arena. In fact it was little more that the floor area of a decent-sized Georgian drawing-room. The two presenters, Ronnie Walsh and John O'Donoghue, seemed to stride across acres of space as they moved from item to item. It was a splendid subterfuge, as they marched, talking into camera but taking minute steps to cover tiny spaces on the crowded studio floor.

We had been brought in to discuss the topic of Irish neutrality (it just shows how little changes). I had a distinguished panel. Fortunately I already knew them all: Liam Cosgrave, former Fine Gael Minister of External

Affairs and subsequently party leader and Taoiseach; Senator Eoin Ryan, whose father had been a founder and noted chairman of Fianna Fáil; the perennially young chronicler and devotee of Irish maritime history, John de Courcy Ireland, still a stalwart advocate of Irish neutrality; and Alec Newman, former editor of *The Irish Times* but by now columnist with the *Irish Press*.

There was little time for preparation; no time for nerves. We plunged into a lively exchange. Then came a point in the discussion when it was natural to put a point to Alec Newman, who was arguing the case for change. Of all the panel, he was the one I knew best; we were working together in the old *Irish Press* and saw each other several times a week. I looked across at him, opened my mouth and realised, in an awful and terrifying moment, that I had no idea of his name. I froze for what seemed an eternity. The silence seemed to be eternal. Then, somehow, in desperation I staggered on with the debate.

It was not just an embarrassing moment; it was an episode of terror. Here I was, on my first outing on the national television service at a time when everything that happened on the television screen was analysed and dissected. And I'd dried up in front of the nation.

But that night I learned two important lessons. One was that embarrassment is something inside ourselves. Sure, I was embarrassed — nobody else took a blind bit of notice. Quite the contrary, they crowded round after the programme with congratulations. I even got a write-up on my début from the television critic of the *Evening Herald*. And never a word about any embarrassment.

The other lesson was equally useful: never do a programme without doing all your homework and, most important of all, no matter how well you know them, always write the names of your guests in bold letters on a card in front of you. That way, for sure, you'll never need to look, but you'll have the security of the information under your nose.

# FRANK FEELY

*Home and Away*

Ah yes, I remember it well.

The scene was San Jose, California — Dublin's sister city. It was a well-attended Irish-American breakfast. I was asked to take the stage and make an impromptu speech. I rabbitted on, making the general point that an occasion which might otherwise be forgettable can become memorable when something goes wrong. I gave a number of examples and finished by referring to a somewhat similar event five years previously when, again in San Jose, I had attended a similar breakfast which was compèred by a beautiful television presenter. When it came to the climax of her speech she said, introducing the Lord Mayor of Dublin, 'And now, ladies and gentlemen, it is my great pleasure to introduce the Right Honourable, the Lord Mayor of London, England.'

As I dismounted from the stage, who did I see approaching me with a steely glint in her eyes but that self same presenter who unbeknownst to me had been in the audience and had spent the intervening years trying to live down her gaffe.

On reflection, I think that a more embarrassing occasion was when I was a 5-year-old pupil in the Presentation Convent, Terenure, I was confronted by a nun. Overcome at being addressed on a one-to-one basis by such an awesome figure — a white face in a sea of black with plastic headpiece and breastplate — I found it hard to concentrate on what she was saying. I did make out 'Go down and tell Miss Fitzsimons', but what I was to tell her did not register. It was unthinkable that I would tell her what she said was indistinct, so I took off down the corridor. Halfway down I stopped, retraced my steps and said to the good Sister, 'She said yes.' On reflection, I think I made the mistake of coming back too soon, but then at 5 years of age one is not all that calculating. It was clear that 'She said yes' was not an appropriate answer anyway.

The nun's reaction was to take off like a bat out of hell down the corridor. She established that I had not in fact delivered the message. When she came back with her face like thunder, she ordered me to sit with the girls. This was a great indignity, especially since the girls had special little chairs with armrests called, if I remember correctly, sugan chairs. To punish me even further she said, 'Girls, don't sit with him', whereupon they and the boys in the class stood around the side of the room, leaving me a lone figure in a sea of vacant chairs. Even this was not enough. She penned a note to my mother to come up the next day to see her.

The following day, my mother duly sought out the nun with me in tow. There followed a rather bewildering scene as they discovered that they were long lost friends who had lost touch, having played together as schoolchildren. My misdemeanour was forgotten, but I shall never forget the embarrassment of sitting alone in disgrace with some fifty children standing around the edge of the class.

# MILDRED FOX

*'Here you go, love. You might need these.'*

Like most politicians, I try to avail of every opportunity to attend functions where there will be large numbers in attendance. Unfortunately, if something goes embarrassingly wrong, you can rest assured that it will not go unnoticed.

St Stephen's Day in Arklow is a day where over a thousand people traditionally turn out to watch a sponsored swim take place in aid of local charities. In 1995 I was invited to take part, and I accepted, though I had never participated in anything of the kind before. My family and friends told me I was stone mad to get into the sea in the middle of winter, but they all sponsored me anyway and even took the precaution of sending somebody from the village to make sure I went through with the swim.

The only person remotely concerned for my health or welfare was my mother who came along for the day with a flask of soup and a couple of towels. Sure enough, it froze hard the night before, and was still below zero on the morning of the swim. I walked down to the edge of the water, towel in hand, complaining how cold it was every two seconds, but there were hundreds of people around, so I smiled even when some of the local 'characters' commented on how purple my legs were.

I decided there was only one way to get this swim over and done with, so I jumped into the water, swam around for about thirty seconds and jumped straight back out. There my cousin held out a neatly rolled towel which I shook out and wrapped around myself. Out of the corner of my eye I thought I noticed something fly past me, but put it down to salty water in my eyes. I then proceeded to push my way back through the crowds along the beach to the car.

Suddenly I heard a man shout after me, so I turned around to see what was wrong. I turned to face a stranger running up the beach waving my underwear in his hand for everyone to see. It suddenly and very painfully dawned on me that my mother had wrapped clean underwear in the towel. 'Here you go, love. You might need these.'

Oh to be an ostrich!

# ROGER GARLAND

In writing this piece I have stretched the meaning of the word 'embarrassing' to include financial embarrassment.

Making a 'book' was, naturally, a strictly forbidden activity at my school. Poker, pitch and toss and smoking were all tolerated, but bookmaking was considered a major sin.

I won't embarrass my old school by mentioning it by name, except to say that it was a boarding school run by the Vincentian Fathers in County Dublin. You may be able to work it out for yourself!

I think I must have been in third year when the opening occurred: the previous incumbent nicknamed Shylock had left at the end of the previous school year. I grabbed the opportunity with both hands. I took bets on everything: racing, soccer, rugby, anything that moved!

Rugby was the big game at school, so the Junior and Senior Schools' cups were the highlights of the school's sporting year. This was a good place to start. Naturally, nearly everyone wanted to back our own teams, which led to a very unbalanced book. I was lucky the first year, because in the earlier rounds against weak teams the odds I offered were very poor. Towards the final stages of the cups, when I reckoned we would lose, I pushed out the odds. We duly lost and I cleaned up. However, there were some nasty side effects. For most cup matches the entire school would descend on Donnybrook to cheer on the teams. Woe betide those who failed to sing the school's victory chants at anything less than full throttle. A hair wash in the loo (we called it the 'jakes') was the usual punishment. When I was standing to win a fiver (a lot of money in the forties) if we lost, it was a little bit difficult to cheer with absolute conviction. I somehow managed to convince the cheer leaders that I would be delighted to lose the fiver.

Bookmaking may seem a simple business, just a matter of chalking up the odds and, if you balance the book, you make a modest profit. However, it's not that simple, as I discovered the following year when I displayed my prices for the Senior cup. One astute schoolmate, now an eminent doctor, asked for odds on all the teams. He spent the whole afternoon in the study hall and worked out a system whereby, by backing all the teams, he would win money no matter who won. As I didn't always get the money up front I couldn't insist that he pay the £20 in advance. When I was inclined to demure, he muttered that I had a reputation of never refusing a bet. Did I want to lose my good name? He hinted menacingly that perhaps a bit of competition would be no harm. Finally, in an expansive gesture he placed his bets in such a way that if one particular school won the cup, I would actually win money. What could I do? My entire future career was at stake. I caved in and duly paid the price. The following year I retained him as a consultant to make sure that the overall book was profitable.

Towards the end of my last year in school, I finally got my come-uppance. The race was the 2,000 Guineas at Newmarket. There were three outstanding horses in the race: you could forget about the rest. So much for the theory, I mused. Life's not like that. One of the three is bound to finish out of the frame. So I laid 40–1 against naming the first three home (in any order). Naturally, most of the money, some of it only three old pence, was on the three favoured horses and, of course, they all finished in the money.

I was shattered. I couldn't believe the result: Palestine, Prince Simon, and Masked Light who only finished a head in front of Master Gunner who would have saved my bacon. Twenty-five quid down — equivalent to £500 today. My grief was palpable and word spread rapidly among the punters that I had got a skinning. I had no option but to ask for time to pay, without having the faintest idea how I was going to find £25.

I decided to have a quiet walk to try to clear my head. As it happens this ramble brought me quite near a deep water-filled quarry. Suddenly, the mob who had been howling for their money, put two and two together and reckoned that I must be going to put an end to my misery. A small deputation was dispatched pronto to try to head me off. They were most sympathetic. I would be given time; I wouldn't be expected to pay in full. To this day, I wonder was this a case of enlightened self-interest or a genuine concern for my well-being — probably a mixture of the two.

A fund-raising committee was set up and a big charity raffle was launched — also against the rules. I wrote some cock-and-bull story to my father, who coughed up a fiver. I borrowed £4. 10s. from the school money-lender, with a promise to pay back a fiver when I could. He was a long time waiting: he got paid out of my twenty-first birthday money! Eventually, when it was all added up, I was able to declare a dividend of thirteen shillings in the pound.

A cautionary tale. The moral is: leave it to the pros like Seán Power!

# CHRIS GLENNON

I nearly died myself the day the man came into the newspaper office to complain about my report on his death.

Already in a state of shock, having been told that the report was, to put it mildly, premature, his appearance was almost fatal — for me.

It happened so innocently and easily. I was a cub reporter with the *Leinster Leader* in Naas, learning the craft under the guidance of editor, Seamus O'Farrell and reporters Sam Weller and Myles O'Mahony.

As a starter, I gathered notes from the districts, still a feature of all provincial papers more than forty years on.

Each Friday I travelled around part of north County Kildare, getting a lift from an old friend, Brian Malone, who did deliveries for a wholesale bottler, P. C. Glennon & Co. (no relation).

On our first stopover at Sallins, less than three miles from the home base of Naas, customers on whom Brian was calling talked about poor Paddy Mahon who hadn't been well and who had 'passed on' the previous night.

I noted the details of how well respected he had been in the area, and his one-time job driving people from Sallins railway station into Naas at a time when cars were scarce.

The 'death' of Paddy was duly recorded in ten lines of the 'Naas Notes' in the next edition of the *Leader*. The paper had hardly hit the shops when I got the dread news: Paddy wasn't dead at all.

It was dread news to a 17-year-old budding reporter — no matter what Paddy thought about the complimentary comments in the ten lines.

It was no consolation to me that, days before the paper appeared, people in Sallins had been so taken in by word-of-mouth reports that a few had turned up for a wake.

Nor was I consoled that a bit of bad luck prevented me from being saved from what I considered a huge mess. My friend, T. P. Hannigan, a typesetter in the *Leader*, lived in Sallins, but that week he had not set the 'Naas Notes'. He knew that the reports of Paddy's death were wrong and could have saved me. That week Charlie Singleton, who lived in Naas, put the 'Naas Notes' in type.

First thing Monday morning I was at the office to admit my mistake to the editor, Mr O'Farrell.

To my surprise he was not horrified. Mr Mahon was joining a distinguished list of international notables who had read premature reports of their deaths.

So, when Paddy Mahon walked in, Mr O'Farrell told him about Mark Twain, Éamon de Valera and others and brought him across to the Fox Hotel for a drink to celebrate his continued good health.

I never wrote another death notice for the *Leader* unless I had actually been to the funeral.

# TONY GREGORY

Although the incident I will recount here took place nearly twenty-six years ago, I still feel the same sense of embarrassment almost as much as the day it happened.

I had just graduated from UCD with a B.A. degree and I was about to start studying for my Higher Diploma in Education. The H. Dip course included several hours' teaching experience.

I combined the need for teaching experience with the need to earn money, so I took a job in one of my local VEC colleges at Gt Denmark Street, just off Parnell Square in the north inner city of Dublin. The teaching hours in the VEC were usually better paid, although the job was tougher particularly for a young teacher starting off.

I made sure I was in plenty of time that first morning. I was, of course, a little apprehensive at the thought of facing a class of more that thirty local inner-city gurriers (like myself only a few years before that). However, I braced myself for the experience and headed up to Denmark Street which was not much more than ten minutes walk from where I lived.

Ironically Denmark Street VEC is only a few doors away from the far more famous Belvedere College. These two schools represented the two tiers of Irish education at the time: Belvedere for the social elite and Denmark Street for the children of the poor.

As I walked up the steps into the school, I straightened my tie (I wore one that morning) and glanced in the reflection of the glass-panelled door to make sure that my recently cut hair was in place. I was all spic and span in my rarely worn suit ready for the fray. I asked the friendly porter where the staff room was. He gestured up to the top of the first flight of stairs.

I opened the staff room door and slipped inside. It was a

very small room and already full with the various teachers all on time for the new term. Several of the teachers turned and glanced to see who had come in and, spotting me, they turned back again and resumed their conversations.

I felt a bit strange standing there and thought it was unusual that no one spoke to me — even to welcome and introduce me to the other members of the staff. After about five minutes of this, I really began to feel ignored and embarrassed. There I was, standing in the corner shuffling my feet, when suddenly the bell rang for the start of class.

The other teachers stopped their conversations and began to get ready to head off to each class. One of them looked at me still standing inside the door.

'What class are you in?' he asked. I took out my timetable and told him I was starting with 1B class and then 3A after that. 'Christ,' he said, 'you're a new teacher. We all thought you were a pupil. The head sometimes sends a kid to wait for him up here if there's a problem or whatever.'

He quickly introduced me to the other teachers who all apologised for seeming to ignore me. I thought to myself, if that's how I appear to the teachers, God only knows what the kids will make of me.

I then headed off to teach my first class.

# DES HANAFIN

In the sixties I was drunk most of the time, and anyone who remembers the sixties wasn't there.

I had a beautiful Mercedes car, and on a Sunday morning it gave me great pleasure to give a begrudging, jealous old madam a lift to Mass. She was very upset with my apparent success, the Mercedes being the example.

One particular Sunday, I collected my passenger for Sunday worship as usual. When Mass was over and having prayed for better fortune, little did I know what lay ahead. As we made our way out of the church, to my total embarrassment I suddenly realised my Mercedes was gone. The HP company had lifted it to my companion's delight.

She then told the whole county and all her cousins in America.

# MARY HARNEY

President Clinton's visit to Ireland last December will be remembered as one of the political highlights of the decade.

In the space of a few short days he managed to inject so much human energy into the search for peace in Northern Ireland. Who can forget the warm reception he received on the Falls Road and on the Shankill — and the huge crowds that came out to meet him at Belfast's City Hall, and at College Green in Dublin?

The President was elevated to almost 'pop star' status. Not since the return of Jack Charlton and our footballing heroes from Italia '90 had College Green seen such a gathering.

President Clinton certainly lived up to his 'billing' (if you'll excuse the pun). In his few days here, he proved himself to be a politician of no little substance, displaying a grasp of the political realities in Northern Ireland which impressed all those who met him.

But apart from the political impact of his visit, I am left with one abiding memory of the few days he spent here. It could be described as 'The Tale of what Harney had up her Sleeve'.

The President and his entourage were due to arrive at the Dáil on Friday afternoon to address members of both Houses of the Oireachtas.

The Taoiseach, the Ceann Comhairle and the leaders of

all the political parties welcomed President Clinton in what's known as the Garden Hall, the room which opens out on to the garden front of Leinster House and Merrion Square.

We stood around chatting and President Clinton took particular interest in the photographs of his predecessors on the wall, President John F. Kennedy and President Ronald Reagan, during their visits to the Dáil. Both men had also addressed a joint sitting of the Dáil and Seanad.

The President was also interested in the bronze of Daniel O'Connell by Andrew O'Connor which is exhibited in the Garden Hall.

I had decided to leave my handbag at home, as they can be a big nuisance for such events. You don't know where to put it when the formalities commence, and you're sure to leave it behind at some stage during the hectic schedule of events in the course of the day. Men don't realise just how easy they have it! Is there no end to the trials and tribulations of the woman party leader?

I hadn't come completely empty handed, though. I held my trusty lipstick up my sleeve. Well, as we stood in the Garden Hall and chatted with the President, my lipstick fell.

President Clinton kindly picked it up, and I'm sure quickly realised I didn't really need it — my face was already bright red with embarrassment!

And, of course, it wasn't as if the event had been witnessed by just a handful of people standing there in the Garden Hall. Hundreds of thousands of people watched the incident on television. And, judging by the number of people who asked me about it, the mystery about what had fallen must have exercised thousands of minds in the following few days.

Was it a fancy handkerchief? Was it a piece of jewellery? What did he say? Were you 'scarlet' with embarrassment? At least, it made a change from all the difficult political questions usually asked of me by people I meet in the course of my duties!

Anyway, I've kept the lipstick as a memento of the

occasion, and am trying to track down some inventor or entrepreneur who might be able to come up with an idea as to how women can carry accessories without having to haul along a handbag to every social occasion. There must be millions to be made out of it. And it could transform my life as a party leader!

# JACK HARTE

*A Bit of Kidnapping*

I have come to the conclusion that true embarrassment is possible only within the context of an accepted code of behaviour. When I look back through the eyes of a writer, I cannot recall a single true embarrassment; when I look back as a teacher and school principal, I find embarrassment at every twist of the way — for example, the thorough haranguing I gave a woman one day about the performance of a student, to discover eventually that she was not the boy's mother but a teacher who had slipped into the queue outside my door in order to give me her CV.

The worst must certainly be the day four of the Sixth Year boys came bursting into my office, breathless.

'Sir, sir, two bikes have been stolen. Two young lads. Gone out the gate. Quick, quick. They've just gone, down the road. We can catch them.'

I leaped up from behind my desk and charged out to the car park, followed by the students. We hopped into my car and burned some rubber, appropriately, as we accelerated off in pursuit.

'Cool customers. Cycled out the front gate, they did. We saw them through the window.'

We zoomed off in the direction they had seen the bicycle thieves go, but quickly came to a cul-de-sac.

'They must have crossed the footbridge down to the dual carriageway. That's the only way they could have gone.

Quick, sir, back to the dual carriageway.'

Round we went, and out on to the dual carriageway. The four students who were with me were all athletic young men. So I issued instructions. Absolute care. Nothing dangerous. I didn't want any injuries, to them or to the lads on the bikes.

About a mile down the road we spotted two young cyclists, pedalling furiously in front of us.

'That's them, that's them. And they're the bikes.'

'All right. We'll take it slowly,' I said, releasing the accelerator, allowing the car to cruise in the slipstream of the cyclists. I waited until the carriageway was clear of traffic, then passed them out and stopped about a hundred yards ahead. The five of us jumped out of the car.

I waved down the two lads, but they ignored me and tried to cycle past. Three of my students grabbed one of them, taking him and the bike in one clean swoop. The other lad shot past, pursued by the fourth of my students who was quickly gaining ground.

The young lad cycled frantically up to a bus stop where there was a huddle of people, threw the bike aside and knelt down in front of them.

'Help me. Help me, please. I'm being kidnapped,' he wailed in a most convincing manner to the bewildered onlookers.

My man was upon him almost immediately and had him firmly apprehended. I went up to the bus queue to reassure them.

'It's OK. I'm a school principal. I know what I'm doing.' They didn't seem too impressed, but they didn't look concerned either.

We bundled the two lads into the back seat, flanked on either side by two of my students, and set off, with the other two proudly cycling the bikes behind the car.

Eventually, one of the terrified lads enquired: 'What are you going to do with us now?'

'Stealing bicycles is very serious,' I replied. 'We'll go back to the school and decide whether to tell your parents or the police.'

'But we didn't steal any bikes. They're our bikes.'

'Your bikes? Didn't you cycle out our front gate on them?'

'Yeah, but we cycled in on them as well. We have the day off in our school and John Sullivan's ma asked us to bring up a message to him.'

'John Sullivan in First Year?'

'Yeah, he lives beside us.'

The shock was like a bullet through the head. By now we had reached the school again. Desperately trying to find a dignified stepping stone out of this morass. No need to summon John Sullivan, or anyone else, to verify the story. I believed them. No way out. Only bluff.

We got out of the car and I called for the two bicycles.

'OK, lads, I'll let you off this time. But don't do it again.'

The relieved youngsters got up on their bikes gingerly, while my Sixth Year students slunk back into class. I waited for the angry phone call, the Garda investigation, the solicitor's letter, the writ, wondering what the headlines would say — 'Principal in Kidnapping Incident'? — wondering what the charge would be — defamation? kidnapping? false imprisonment?

But the bluff worked. I heard no more about it. When you're a principal it's easy to make youngsters feel guilty. And they never dream of thinking it's you that's got it all wrong.

# SEAN HAUGHEY

Recently I met with my wife's best friend and congratulated her on her engagement to Paul. No sooner were the words out of my mouth when I realised that something was wrong. I found out a short time later that in actual fact she had broken up with

Paul about a year earlier and was now in fact engaged to Kevin. Never mind. These things happen.

A public representative who is out and about meeting people all day long very often has to deal with the unpredictable and can be asked to say a few words at very short notice. He has, therefore, many opportunities to put his foot in it.

As Lord Mayor of Dublin, I thanked on stage the director of the Amateur Musical and Dramatic Society, Mrs Olive Jones, in front of a crowd of 300, for the crucial role she played in producing the performance that evening, which I recall was 'The Pied Piper of Hamlin'. Instantly, I realised that the audience had become uneasy as the murmur in the hall became louder and louder. Oops . . . actually the director's name was Mrs Olive O'Brien. In these situations one soon learns to move swiftly on to the next business.

Personnel from every visiting foreign navy ship to the Port of Dublin pay a courtesy visit to the Lord Mayor. One particular day naval officers from a French Navy ship in the company of Irish officers called to the Mansion House. In the course of the conversation, I innocently asked if the Greenpeace ship which had been at the same berth the previous day had since moved on. To my horror, I suddenly remembered the role of the French Navy in the destruction of the Greenpeace ship, the *Rainbow Warrior*. Cups began to rattle as the serving house steward, in horror, almost dropped the silver tea tray. The question remained unanswered as the subject was changed as quickly as possible.

We all have embarrassing moments. One should not dwell on them, but rather turn the page, put them behind us and start again.

# LIAM HAYES

'**I**'m going to tell you everything once, and let's do it! I don't want to have to tell you twice.'

The weeks before a Leinster football final were always the toughest weeks of the year. On the Meath team everybody was tense, uptight and prone to take the heads off one another — just for the hell of it.

Actually, the reason we were all in a bad mood was Dublin! The Dublin football team always cast that spell over the Meath team in the late 1980s. It was never any fun for us playing against Dublin. We always wanted to beat them so badly. Football by mid-July of each year was a very serious business indeed.

On this particular night, two weeks before the final, Sean Boylan was the bear with the sorest head of all! None of us knew why he was in such awful form, and nobody asked.

It was lashing rain all day long, and the evening was dark and miserable, the worst evening of the year to date, but strangely it probably suited the mood of the team perfectly. Maybe Sean just wanted to get in out of the heavy rain. Maybe he had just had a very bad day at work. God knows.

Anyhow, we were doing the usual things, the usual ball exercises in the middle of the field for the first twenty or thirty minutes. Then, Sean brought us over to one sideline and divided us all up into groups of four.

We all knew what he had in mind — the toughest, most painful, unmerciful exercise of all!

Obviously he had chosen it with this horrible evening in mind. He had placed six balls on the ground ten yards from the sideline, and in pairs at the sound of his whistle we had to sprint out and get them. One on one! Whoever got the ball first, and wasn't rammed into the ground by his opponent as he tried to pick the ball up, had to bring the ball back to the sideline, hopping and soloing. His opponent was a defender. And, if his opponent dispossessed him, then they automatically assumed each other's role. Either way, someone had to get the ball back to the sideline! And everybody was going to end up totally ballocksed within ten or fifteen minutes!

It's a grinding and tiring exercise and everybody hates it, and I knew Sean had it in mind. Before he said anything further, I started taking my wet suit top off, pulling it over my shoulders. I ran over to Padraig Lyons, who was injured and was hunched underneath an umbrella beside one of the balls. Padraig said something to me, and I answered him as Sean began to say something.

I'd missed what Sean said. 'What's that?' I shouted. He was furious.

'What did I say? I want everything done fast! I'm not going to say everything twice!'

I was wet and tired, and innocent (I was taking a top off) and before I knew it, I had said it: 'I didn't fucking hear you!'

Everyone else was silent, the bastards, happy with the breather and the bit of entertainment. They watched Sean marching over to me. I couldn't believe it. He took off the whistle which had been hanging around his neck on a piece of string, and he threw the damn thing at my feet.

'OK, you want to take charge — you take charge!'

'Jesus, don't do that,' I replied. He was already walking away in a huff. 'I didn't hear you,' I added. I had my hands on my hips and I was still soaked right through, and I felt like a total idiot. I picked up the whistle, walked over to Sean and handed it over to him.

That made me feel a bigger idiot still. I don't know what Sean felt. He was still fuming. It was still raining. Everybody else was dying to start laughing — but they didn't dare. Not until afterwards.

'How's it going, coach?' Bob O'Malley asked, as he passed by towards the showers. Colm O'Rourke also had to say something, typically, great friend that he is!

'If you weren't so thick, and if you'd any sense, you'd have taken the fucking whistle.' And he also had words for Sean Boylan. 'I wouldn't take that from these young lads, Sean.'

# ALISON HEALY

*Close Encounters of the Road Kind*

For some strange reason, all my embarrassing moments seem to centre around the car and my close encounters on the road. The characters in the 'X Files' almost seem sane and well adjusted when you compare them with the individuals I have met, behind the wheel.

Perhaps this is a sad indictment on my driving? I cannot imagine that this is the case. Doesn't every learner driver spend more time in the ditch observing the flora and fauna than on the road during that first tentative year of driving?

Anyway, this particular moment, like all truly embarrassing moments, still makes me cringe today, years after it happened.

I was a young learner driver in a truculent Polo which had the unnerving habit of dancing across the M50 whenever a gentle breeze blew. On this day I was on one of my first assignments as a nervous trainee journalist. It was one of those rows between residents and the county council. After a great number of telephone calls, I had finally tracked down a resident who reluctantly agreed to talk to me, so I was driving to meet him.

I was tripping along in the fast lane on a dual carriageway, lost in reverie, when I heard a loud toot of a horn behind me. I was completely in the wrong and acknowledged this, moving in quickly to give way to him. That was fine and he continued down the fast lane.

Now the slow lane was moving more quickly, and a stream of cars, including mine, passed him by. He seemed to take a personal affront to this as he suddenly shot into the slow lane behind me and started to flash his lights and toot his horn. This was a new experience for me. First of all, I thought that maybe I knew him. Just in case I did, I gave a slight wave.

To my horror, he started to gesticulate, hitting his head wildly. Then he passed me out, blowing his horn constantly as he went. Well, that was really quite enough. A sensible person might have said good riddance and let him go, but I was furious at this stage. Learner driver or not, this was no way to treat someone on the road. Summoning all the power in the 957 cc Polo, I revved up and finally reached him. He was still in the fast lane and I was in the slow lane.

Now I must warn you that the following behaviour is completely alien to me. I drew level with him and kept level for a moment, to make sure that he saw me. Then I passed him out, and in a most glorious and defiant gesture, I threw my two fingers up at him as I sailed by. Being a fairly mild-mannered and polite person, I was surprised at how good this made me feel.

My only fear was that he would come after me, foaming at the mouth, chase me and the unfortunate Polo into the ditch and relentlessly pursue me across the fields. I would surely break one of the heels on my shoes in this dramatic chase, I thought. Happily this didn't happen and I eventually reached the town unharmed.

After numerous forays in housing estates, I finally found the right address. In my haste to get to the interview, I pushed the bell too hard and it stuck, ringing loudly and incessantly. Just as I was trying to release it, the door opened. The man looked strangely familiar. The bell continued to ring as the dreadful realisation sank in. I looked at the car sitting in the driveway. Yes, I was standing face to face with the man I had just thrown my fingers up at. Not only that, he had to dismantle his bell to stop it ringing.

That was certainly not one of my best interviews.

# MARY HENRY

Many years ago I had occasion to be in County Wicklow at a meeting. It was one of those glorious summers and it was very difficult to be indoors all day. However, our meeting ended earlier than planned and someone suggested we go to Brittas Bay for a swim. I declined as I had no bathing suit with me. Unfortunately (I say this on hindsight), my excuse was not accepted and before I could protest again a white bathing suit was thrust at me. Somebody had a spare one and lent it to me. So off we went.

When we got there I was delighted that I had agreed to the suggestion. The sun was still splitting the stones and the sea was blue and inviting. We all togged out and ran enthusiastically into the water, splashing and jumping and running back out again because, as is usual in Irish waters, it was freezing. However, eventually we were all in and frolicking around.

After about ten minutes I decided I had had enough and so headed back towards the place where we had left our clothes. I noticed people looking at me. Can you imagine the shock and horror I felt when I realised that the bathing suit I was wearing was totally transparent? But there was nothing I could do. There was nowhere to hide. The distance back to my clothes seemed like a thousand miles. Eventually I got there and my embarrassment only served to provide great hilarity among my friends.

Since then, however, whenever I am buying a bathing suit, I check it, double check it and check it again so that my most embarrassing moment will never be repeated.

# JONATHAN IRWIN

*Stoned at the Dome*

A couple of years ago I happened to be in Los Angeles for a race meeting at Santa Anita. The racing came and went. The international horsemen left town and I had two days to kill. Somehow I found out that Noel Pearson was in town and I rang him to ask him to lunch with me at Le Dome. Noel has always ranked among my truer friends and one to be cherished since he broke new ground by agreeing to bring *Joseph* to Goffs and play it in the Round in 1976. Not only was it a brilliant production directed by Alan Simpson and featuring Noel Purcell in one of his last performances, but it paid more than one of Goffs bills that year. It was such a smash ('Musical of the Year') that it just ran and ran, and if it hadn't been for the National Irish Yearling Sale in September it might have run till Christmas. If Pearson is a friend for all seasons, he also happens to be a truly entertaining companion.

Rather like *Joseph*, lunch ran and ran until there was only one other table left. The host at that table for two turned out to be David Gilor who produced *Alien* and whom I'd met a number of times in London. In the way these things happen he and the girl lunching with him found our table. Noel and David disappeared into the world of show business talk, leaving me with an understated, charming and witty partner. I remember thinking that rather than the usual painful brashness of Los Angeles, here was a truly unspoilt simple girl who seemed interested in breaking into films. Suddenly I realised my role — knight in armour, sunlight breaking through the forest glade, and damsel delivered to Oscar-winning producer Noel Pearson. Remembered forever, I would show to my grandchildren photographs of a great star discovered by grandfather. As soon as Noel drew breath I bounced my wild idea on him. As his eyes clouded over, I wondered how could this genius not understand my natural ability as an agent.

David and the damsel left, and as they disappeared with the twilight of Beverly Hills, Noel leant across: 'I sense you've no idea who the girl was?' 'No,' I replied. 'Sharon Stone, ya ballocks!'

# EDDIE KEHER

*The Unexpected Invited Guests!*

Young people would find it hard to imagine it now, but those of us who got married in the sixties will be very familiar with the early days of homemaking that I am about to describe.

Nowadays, when young people get married, they have their house fully carpeted, curtains on all the windows and the house fully furnished before their wedding day.

In the sixties we were very happy to have the four walls of our house when we came back from the honeymoon. By scrimping and saving, pieces of furniture were added, and bit by bit each room was fitted out during the early years of marriage.

There were the bare floors, and we had to improvise with orange boxes, stools, etc. until a kitchen suite was affordable, and likewise for the other rooms of the house.

Antiquated and frugal as it may seem in today's world, there was enjoyment and excitement as each part of the house began to take shape.

While the cooker was an early essential for the kitchen, a fridge had to be placed way down the line on the list of priorities. As a result, there was never a stock of food, only the day-to-day requirements.

There was very little money left over for the kind of socialising that is taken for granted today, and a night out was a visit to other newly married friends to compare notes and see how their orange boxes were surviving!

On one occasion I met an acquaintance in town, and on parting, I invited him and his wife to visit us. To suit both of us, we had to decide on a night about two weeks away. I forgot to tell Kay, my wife, of the arrangement and, in the intervening period, I forgot completely about the invitation myself!

On the night in question, we were doing a bit of painting when the door bell rang, and I went down to answer. When I saw the couple at the door, I was so engrossed in the painting it did not even dawn on me then that I had issued an invitation. I assumed that it was just a casual call (which was always a possibility in those days).

There was the usual amount of scrambling to get the place and ourselves organised. The night was going grand, until I suddenly remembered that I had actually invited the couple. Kay was completely oblivious to the fact as she went to prepare supper. She assumed that she was 'playing a blinder' by being able to produce cream crackers and cheese with sliced orange to go with the coffee for this unexpected call.

When the guests left, and I told her, she nearly died of embarrassment. Suffice to say, I was presented with a diary the next day to make sure all arrangements were recorded.

We both regard that incident as our most embarrassing moment, and we still cringe when we think of it.

I am sure the very understanding couple were aware of what happened, but did their best not to embarrass us at the time. It was one of those incidents where you would act differently if it happened again; but maybe my writing it down in print, so many years later, will help us not to cringe every time we think of it!

# JIM KEMMY

*Memories of Moving Statues*

Reading recent reports about milk-drinking statues in India and other places brought painful memories back to my mind of our own moving-statue phenomenon of the wretched summer and autumn of 1985. Like everybody else, it took me some time to recover from the initial surprise. As a stonemason and public representative, I tried to stand back from the moving statues, but soon these events took over a centre-stage role in the nation's affairs.

Soon, large crowds began to flock to Ballinspittle, Mount Melleray, Asdee, Ballydesmond, Courtmacsherry, Garryowen, and a few locations in my native city of Limerick. Burger and chip vans and mobile shops of all kinds rolled into place to service the swelling hordes. Television and radio programmes, newspaper and magazine articles and a variety of books followed on. Meanwhile, I continued to keep my head down and my gaze averted from the passing parade of the embarrassing and rapidly increasing number of statues.

Eventually the media realised that I, given my building background, might know something about statues, and I was forced to come to terms with the subject publicly. I gave a measured and matter-of-fact interview to a local journalist, during which I stated that after more than thirty years' experience in handling such materials as stone, concrete and plaster, I was not aware of any chemical process by which these inanimate objects could assume the powers of locomotion. I further ventured to suggest that the phenomenon was a turning away from reality and said that I had no reason to believe that — contrary to the then current predictions — the end of the world was at hand. Most of the contents of the interview were reprinted a few days afterwards in the *Evening Press*.

My entry into the affair provoked controversy. People were divided on the issue: some felt that the statues were being moved through divine intervention and that my response had been too dogmatic; others believed that I had given a fair reply. But I had not counted on the vigilant editorial writer in the *Tipperary Star* weighing in heavily behind the moving statues. In its issue of 28 September 1985, it carried this front page leading article, titled 'Moving Statues'.

Limerick Socialist Mr Jim Kemmy is nothing if not controversial and this week he again rushes in where even bishops fear to tread, on the 'phenomenon' of the moving statues, attributing the recent events to a 'turning away from reality'. A strange choice of words indeed, having regard to the fact that the hundreds of thousands of people who have been flocking to shrines all over the country might, more correctly, be said to be turning *towards* reality rather than away from it — According to Mr Kemmy 'We should turn towards life, towards young people and find some answers, ourselves, to our problems.' By all accounts, anybody who has been to any one of the shrines that have been mentioned in recent months, must surely have noticed that this is exactly what so many people *are* doing: and to judge again, from reports, they would seem to have found at least some 'answers to their problems' — perhaps not yet the jobs they seek nor even the weather Mr Kemmy and the rest of us would like to have, but a certain fulfilment which, at least, helps them to cope a little better with these problems.

And as I read the content, I felt like the Czar of Russia when the *Skibbereen Eagle* turned its baleful eye on him!

I received many copies of this editorial from Tipperary readers. As I contemplated the article, another editorial, this time in the *Limerick Leader* of 5 October 1985, was published under the heading, 'The Afterline':

And so it did come to pass. The prophets of doom in Limerick had predicted that the world would end on 28 September. But last Saturday came and went without so much as a whiff of brimstone. Now, perhaps, we can all resume learning to live with reality . . . always assuming, of course, that we can avoid being hit by moving statues.

Learning to live with reality is not always easy, and perhaps I should be grateful that I was 'hit' by the *Tipperary Star* and not by a moving statue! But the moving statues had achieved one almost miraculous result. At long last, after many more years than I care to remember, the *Leader's* editorial writer and myself had found common cause. This was surely a phenomenal and moving experience!

In the last decade many writers have reflected on the matter. In her article, 'Moving Statues and Irish Women', published in the *Women's Studies Reader* in 1993, Margaret MacCurtain quotes Mary Holland in trying to explain what went on. 'The crowds at Ballinspittle dramatise the problem facing the Church . . . for the yearning after the old certainties goes beyond religious practice to reflect the unease with the quality of life in Ireland and with a society which . . . has failed them materially as well as spiritually.' She also quoted the folklorist, Dáithí Ó hÓgáin: 'It would seem to be of far greater value if we searched for the underlying causes which lead people to notice such things at some times and places than others.' Margaret MacCurtain concluded:

> For many Irish Catholics there was perplexity. To a society as highly sacramentalised as the Catholic Irish, new demands of vernacular liturgy resulting from a changed model of Church caused bewilderment. There was a sense of loss which affected devotional practice and religious observance alike. It is in this period that Professor J. A. Murphy, a specialist in twentieth-century Irish history, perceives 'a collapse of the kind of solid Catholic church-going practices that were there up to 1960 or so'.

This is as near as we are likely to get to understanding why statues were believed to be on the move in 1985. And, of course, the terrible summer of that year did not help to dispel the spiritual mood of doom and gloom. My difference of opinion with the *Tipperary Star* did not change the world, but I cannot look back on the year 1985 without a rush of painful memories.

# BRENDAN KENNELLY

I was about to give a lecture entitled 'The Essence of Romanticism' to a group of students in Swarthmore College, Pennsylvania, back in the early 1970s. At home, my 2-year-old daughter loved sitting on my shoulders and being jogged up and down. Shortly before the lecture I took her on my shoulders, held her hands, and as I jogged her up and down she vomited all over my head and shoulders. Handing my daughter back to her mother, I tried to clean myself as best I could. I did. As I spoke about the essence of romanticism, I got the delightful if somewhat unusual perfume of my daughter's vomit from, it seemed, every quarter of my person. To this day, I wonder if the students got it too!

Since then, I've never doubted that I'm a true romantic!

# BENEDICT KIELY

One day, some years ago, a newspaper editor asked me if I could write down for him, and his readers, I presumed, any memories I had of those days of wrath, those dreadful days, on which, so long ago, myself and the other gurriers went back to school after the summer holidays.

So, I sat down in a dark corner and gave the matter serious thought and found that, although I have a fair memory when I try, I could not remember a damned one of those days. 'Damned' is exactly the word I was searching for.

Psychiatrists tell us that we are inclined to forget matters that we find unpleasant to remember. And the great horse-rider, Lester Pigott, came up with one of the wisest remarks of all time when he said that the only thing he ever learned at school was that you had to go there. What little boy Lester wanted to learn could not be taught in a classroom.

Nowadays, I can never see a chiseller creeping like a snail, not so much unwillingly as uncomprehendingly, to school, without my thinking of Lester Pigott.

Yet, if I have now found that I cannot remember a day on which I was supposed to go back to school, I find also that I do remember a day when I went back to school, by accident, and when I was supposed to be going to work for my living and for the first time.

Incidentally, a lovely lady who went to college with me had, in relation to the use of that word 'supposed', a theory that our own beloved Ireland is a vast supposition and may not, in truth, exist at all. Everyone in Ireland, she argued, is supposed to be doing something or being somewhere or, not infrequently, supposed to be doing something else or being somewhere else. Just listen hard any day and count how often you hear the word 'supposed' used. And even how often you yourself use it.

Anyway, that day when I went back to school, when I was supposed to be going to work, is so tied up with the personality of a man long dead, a great teacher. He was a Clare man by birth, from the lovely town of Kilkee. He was a graduate of one of the great English universities: I forget which. He taught, or tried to teach, Latin and English to myself and a lot of other young gentlemen whose heart may not really have been in literature, ancient or modern. He was one of those teachers, and they're not all that common, who became a legend to the generations. He taught men who, if they are or were still around, would now be 90-plus years of age. He died suddenly in 1939. His initials were M. J. His wife, I know, called him Michael. But we knew him simply, and when he wasn't listening, as Joe.

He was not the sort of man who would acquire a more elaborate or caricaturing nickname because he had, first and before all things, an awe-inspiring presence. Not that he was violent or severe. He was just so unmistakably there: six feet and a bit more in height, broad shouldered. He had been an amateur boxer in one of the heavier weights, and one arm, cracked in conflict, was forever slightly bent. He dressed always in dark suits, with a pinstripe, and wore strong expensive well-polished boots. He wore rimless spectacles with a little golden chain attached to the right ear. He had gone more or less bald and what hair he had he combed forward, and kept frequently combing it with the fingers of his right hand as he walked the classroom, never raising his voice immoderately, but talking firmly, persuading us that not only was a little learning not a dangerous thing, but that it might even be of benefit to us in the life that lay ahead.

It will all be the same in a hundred years, he would say. But in the meantime you might, for a while, like to read a book, or even to eat and have a house to live in.

He loved literature even to the point of lending us his own books in the hope that we would read and appreciate, and return, them. That's always a hazardous confidence to place in students. Yet, I don't think any of us ever let him down and he had his own humorous way of reminding us if the end of term approached and the books were still unaccounted for. He would look at the class silently for a few minutes, twisting his lips wryly, the light glistening off his spectacles. He was the great master of the pregnant silence. Then he would solemnly announce: 'Let down the windows and bring me back my books.'

One particularly bad borrower did bring back a book on the very last day of term, walked boldly up the classroom, placed the book on the master's desk, and walked back again to his seat. Nobody made a sound. Outside the window the sun shone on the convent field, where the pet brown donkey that the neighbouring Loreto nuns kept in honour of Bethlehem grazed in content. Then the master said: 'Jeff, a mission in your parish? Is it the Redemptorists? Strong men.'

In those days the students who came in by train or bus, or even by bicycle, from rural corners and country towns, used to bring their little parcels of bread with them to eat at lunchtime in a restaurant where they could get a cup of tea for a penny. The simple life — and no mistake! But it often happened that hunger would overtake some poor devil in mid-morning and he'd begin to munch, with what secrecy he could muster in the crowded classroom. Once, a decent boy from the town of Fintona had his mouth as full as it could hold when that same silence, awesome but never evil because humour was always there, descended on the room. Then came the question: 'Colm, what are you chewing?'

There was a sudden, agonised swallow.

'My lunch, sir.'

'Continue, Colm. It was just that for one worried moment I thought it was the cud.'

Then he had the most wonderful ways of catching a half-sleeping student with a silly question and waking him up to laugher but never to recrimination. He would read out dramatically some poetical fragment:

> For often in O'Connor's van
> To triumph dashed each Connacht clan. . . .

A silence, then, 'Tell me, James, what were they doing always racing around in that old van?'

Or reading, out loud, from William Morris, how Svend and his brethren built great roads that over their smooth surfaces the wains might go, he might pause to ask a slumberer if the weans at that time had nowhere to play except on the roads.

Or on the highest level of all he might read Bolingbroke's complaint of how his enemies had maltreated him:

> From out my windows torn my household coat,
> Razed out my impresse, leaving me no sign
> Save men's opinions, and my living blood,
> To show the world I am a gentleman.

The silence. And then the question: 'Tell me, Michael, were the Bolingbrokes so poorly off that they had to keep an old coat stuffed in the window?'

One day, he sent me out to the cloakroom to get from his overcoat pocket a copy of G. K. Chesterton's *The Flying Inn* which he had promised, against his own judgment, to lend to me. 'In the right pocket,' he said, 'my cigarette butts. Leave them be. In the left pocket, your friend, Mr Chesterton.' The Chestertonian paradox, oddly enough, did not appeal to him. Perhaps it was too close to the comic side of himself. And he practically despised Belloc for those articles during the First World War in *Land and Water*, in which Belloc had kept forecasting the downfall of Prussia; and that downfall kept obstinately postponing itself. Yet in days when Bernard Shaw and others were making monumental fools, or worse, out of themselves, on such subjects as the efficiency of Hitler, this Clare man teaching school in an Ulster town spoke, in and out of season, against Hitler and Mussolini. One of the more notable diversions in class was his gentle but firm argufying with a friend of mine who professed to be pro-Mussolini for the odd, or perhaps not so odd, reason that his elder brother was in the Irish College in Rome.

And the last letter from that great man and teacher came to me a week before he dropped dead on the Courthouse Hill on the High Street of Monaghan town. That letter contained a dire and accurate prophecy of the horrors to come in the Hitler War.

But, about that day on which I set off to work in the local

post office and went instead, absentmindedly, to school.

He was out smoking and sunning himself before classes, and we laughed uproariously at my mistake. Then he brought out the great brown suitcase he carried his gear in, took out a book and gave it to me. He said, 'Oddly enough, I felt you might be here today. So I brought this along.'

And as I walked away, to be late for work on my very first day as a wage-labourer, he called after me: 'Write and tell me what you think of that book. Stick to the books and you'll go far.'

Years later, when I was on the far side of the ocean and a continent, and talking about books to young people in the University of Oregon, I'd pause in the middle of a talk and see him, the pin-striped suit, the glint on his eye-glasses, the wry smile on his lips, and I'd hear him say: 'I told you so, didn't I? Look out over the Pacific. Go any further and you'll soon be on the road home.'

And I had written and told him what I thought of that book. And it dawned on me afterwards that he had subtly walked me into writing my first book review.

And, I daresay, I stuck to the books, as best I could.

# HUGH LEONARD

Where the dropping of bricks is concerned, I can say with hand on heart that I have never in my life put my foot in it. It has always been both feet or nothing. There was, for example, the day when I came out of our local newsagent's to discover that a young man was sitting on the bonnet of my car. 'I'm sorry,' I said to him, 'that I can't offer you a chair!' He made no reply, simply picked up his crutches, tucked them under his arms and hobbled off.

And I cannot recall without blushing how, as a teenager, I sat on a bench on the Dun Laoghaire sea front next to a middle-aged couple. I was reading a book and, out of the corner of my eye, saw that an elderly and poorly dressed man was standing in front of me. I paid him no attention and, after a while, he poked at me with his finger. I had no money, not even for my own bus fare home, never mind to give to a beggar, so I ignored him. Undaunted, he continued to poke at me with his finger.

At last, as angry with myself as with him, I all but shouted, 'I have no money to give you!' At this the woman who was sitting next to me said, 'The man only wants you to move up so's he can sit down.' I fled.

Once, a well-known Irish writer, then living in Paris, wrote — in longhand, not typescript — to decline my invitation that he should come to Dublin to see my stage adaptation of one of his novels. The reason he gave was 'my mortgage has broken down'. I wrote to him to say that poverty should not keep him away, that I was prepared to send him his air fare and to put him up at a modest guesthouse, even buy him dinner.

I sent this letter off, feeling virtuous, if not downright saintly. Then I looked again at *his* letter. What he had written was that his *marriage* had broken down.

Worst of all was the day I was sitting in the office of the film producer, Jules Buck, when none other than Sophia Loren came in, accompanied by her husband, Carlo Ponti. Introductions were quickly made, then she said to Mr Buck: 'Jules, I can't thank you enough for my new wig. It's wonderful . . . don't you think so?'

I looked at her and put in my own ha'pennyworth. 'Yes,' I said, 'it's beautiful'.

She said: 'Thank you, but I'm not wearing it now.'

# SAM MCAUGHTRY

When I joined the RAF after the outbreak of war I was taken to Padgate, a huge receiving centre, to be medically examined, sworn in, vaccinated, inoculated, dentally treated, kitted out with a uniform and given bedding, blankets and sheets.

It was the sheets that caused the trouble. The corporal in charge of our hut mustered us all together: 'Have you all got everything?' he enquired. Everybody around me shouted: 'Yes, corporal.'

'And so you're all happy?'

'Yes, corporal.'

Me? I was nervous. I wasn't so happy. But I wasn't used to speaking up in a crowd of strangers and I envied the Britishers who seemed to have no bother at all with it. But something was worrying me. Hesitantly, I raised my hand. 'Yes?' the corporal said.

'It's these sheets.' I had to clear my throat halfway through the delivery. 'Right, Paddy.' The corporal had my tongue taped right away. I was to learn that all we Irish, from North and South both, were Paddies. British corporals didn't know about King Billy.

'Yes, come on, Paddy, let's be having you. What about the sheets?' The corporal was beside me now.

'Well, I've got two of them, look. Could you take one back?'

I'd never slept between two sheets in my life, and I didn't know that there was a class of people who did. In Cosgrave Street, Belfast, we didn't even have real sheets, just flour bags, opened out and stitched together. Sometimes we didn't even have those — just the rough itch of the blankets to lie on.

The corporal stared, then he burst out laughing, and, on hearing him, so did some of the recruits: 'You dim Irish twit,' the corporal shouted, 'what kind of a turnip-basher are you?'

I went first of all red from the embarrassment, then redder from the insult. I dropped my bedding on the ground: 'This sort of a turnip-basher,' I shouted, letting a left hook loose. It kind of scorched his neck as he swerved. He must have been a bit of a scrapper.

They told me it was a record. I received seven days confined to barracks on my first day in the service. It would have been more, the squadron leader told me, only, hearing my side of it, he understood something of my background. I learned later that he was Irish. Not having been further than Bangor in County Down before joining up, I couldn't tell the upper-class Southern accent.

It wasn't doing the CB and kitchen fatigues that made the incident the most embarrassing of my life — it was the way that they all laughed. I took it as an insult to our family, our street, and to the whole of Tiger's Bay. But anyway, for the rest of the time that I was there, nobody laughed at me again.

# JIM McCANN

*From the Jaws of Death*

When I was invited to contribute an item for this book, several stories sprang immediately to mind. On mature reflection (as the politicians say) I realised that this book will possibly be read by people of a nervous, sensitive or even religious disposition. The following story, therefore, is the highest on my list which shouldn't offend anybody. I, however, still bear the mental scars.

When I was young, our family holidayed every year in Achill Island — idyllic times which I still remember fondly. With the exception of one day!

On that fateful day, my cousin and I were having great fun swimming and diving off a small jetty near where we were staying. I think it was called Dugort. The day before, we had all gone up to the heights overlooking Keem Bay, and with delicious dread had watched the enormous shapes of huge basking sharks lazily rounding the headland and disappearing again out to sea. Although our parents had assured us that these sharks were harmless vegetarians, we chose to think of these behemoths as prehistoric monsters of the kind that haunt childish nightmares! Huddled in bed that night, we breathlessly imagined our fate should we be caught by one of these terrible creatures.

Anyway, on the day in question our fun on and off the jetty had us in uproarious good humour, which made what followed all the more terrifying! With many a cry of 'Look at me' to the assembled crowd of kids on the small beach (most of whom were, of course, little girls — some things never change) I performed a beautiful forward somersault into the water and landed on — a shark!

Seemingly I literally screamed, actually shrieked in terror. I say 'seemingly' because my brain wasn't functioning, but there was no shortage of grinning witnesses to describe the scene to me afterwards. I ran, still screaming, on to the beach *along the surface of the water*! As God was their judge, they swore that I was going too fast to sink. A group of adults ran up, alarmed by the commotion, and these included a pair of burly fishermen. When the situation was explained, they roared with laughter and forcibly escorted me back out on the jetty, where they hauled from the water a 12 foot basking shark. A *dead* basking shark! They'd tied it under the water to keep it from 'going off'.

It must have been a slow week on the island, newswise, because before the day was out everyone had a version of my humiliation. I will carry to my grave the memory of the ridicule I suffered from the other kids, who were thrilled to have a stick to beat the show-off with. And the name-calling! The mildest was 'Moby Dick'.

I thank God that this happened long before the film *Jaws* was spawned, otherwise I know what nickname I'd have been stuck with, probably for the rest of my life.

# MICK MCCARTHY

I was playing for Glasgow Celtic and on my first tour with Ireland. You know how it is — you don't know anyone; you're trying to make a good impression and not do anything wrong, particularly as a new member of the squad.

Everything seemed to be going quite well. I played my début in Poland and was getting to know the lads.

We then went on tour to Japan and were due to play against a Brazilian team called SC International. The trip had gone well to date, we'd done the male bonding bit and I'd not been caught out too often.

The stadium where the match was to be played had a track with a little white rim around it. I'd been out earlier to warm up and everything went OK. There was a huge buzz in the place as we came out for my match. The crowd was roaring. I pranced out, looking the business, and fell flat on my face, straight over the rim. And there I lay, sprawled out on the track, thinking, I've just gone base over apex on to the pitch!

All the lads saw me and gave me a terrible slagging afterwards. It certainly put a stop to my gallop I can tell you. I was suitably chastened and red faced. Not only that. There must have been at least 500 Japanese lads and lassies focused on this great Irish soccer star spreadeagled before them on the pitch and they were having a great laugh at my expense. I didn't need to understand the language to know what they were saying.

Talk about good impressions! Never again — I hope!

# TOM MCCAUGHREN

*Getting Flowery*

I don't know whether I should tell this story, it's so embarrassing. The only excuse I can make is that I have always suffered from hay fever.

I first discovered that I suffered from this condition when I was a boy helping on the farm next door. There was never any shortage of willing young hands when it came to bringing in the hay. That was great fun. If we weren't helping to hold the horse steady, we were helping to crank the haystacks up on to the flat cart. Then we would hitch a ride back down the lane to the barn, where we would jump and roll around in the hay and generally act the eejit as we helped spread each forkful that was thrown up to us. However, I soon discovered that the high jinks in the barn weren't for me. Before long, I would be suffering violent sneezing, a runny nose and watery eyes, and then for several days the equivalent of a very bad cold.

As I grew up, I also discovered that the dust of the hay barn wasn't the only thing that would trigger a bout of hay fever. I suffered similar symptoms from the dust from old papers or books, a draught from an open window, new-mown grass, perfume . . . flowers. Various medicines to try and cure the problem became a feature of my life. As a result, I don't, for example, sniff flowers, and if they are brought into the house, I try and keep my distance from them.

So, you might ask, what is embarrassing about that? Many people suffer from the same condition. Well, it wasn't until my wife was involved in a car crash that the problem arose. Her friends were very concerned about her and were very good to her. Some brought her flowers, and one bunch in particular stood out above all the rest. They were, I think, some kind of lily. They were beautiful, but even though I kept my distance from them, I thought they gave off an awful smell. So much so, that when the Gardaí rang to say they would be calling to take a statement from my wife, I removed the flowers and opened the windows to let the smell out.

It was the same when our friend May called. She was offering my wife words of comfort about the accident when I opened the sitting-room door. The smell of the flowers immediately assailed my nose. 'Sorry about those flowers, May,' I said. 'They've an awful smell. Here, let me take them out.' May didn't reply, but my wife, I could see, was squirming as she tried to send me some kind of signal. 'Tom,' she managed to say between gritted teeth, 'May brought me those flowers.'

What happened next I can't recall with any degree of clarity. What could I say? I do remember muttering something about my hay fever and hearing May laughing as I beat a hasty retreat. It was, I know, very generous of her to laugh it off and, indeed, she has told us often since how heartily she laughed at my embarrassment as she drove home.

Nevertheless, many resolutions followed that moment's embarrassment . . . Must learn to keep my mouth shut, mind my own business, speak only when you're spoken to. None of them, of course, has eased my embarrassment. The only thing that has done that is the knowledge that May laughs every time she thinks about it. Needless to say, my wife doesn't think it was a bit funny!

# CHARLIE McCREEVY

Could a carpenter work without his saw? Can a bricklayer function without his trowel? Impossible, you will agree.

And, likewise, no politician could function without his/her voice. It's elementary — imagine a parliament with your TDs staring at one another and not a sound uttering from any of them! Not even the resonant Tipperary rounded vowels of the Ceann Comhairle's 'Order. Order.'

No more programmes like 'Questions and Answers' with politicians screaming inanities at one another. Sure, think of the unemployment it would cause alone.

Well, as a politician I have experienced many embarrassing moments. As one with a very distinctive voice, it's hard to believe that I once suffered total voice loss while addressing a public meeting.

An occasional laryngitis sufferer, I would have been forewarned on many occasions when the dreaded bug was in its embryonic stages — and corrective action would be taken. But there was no such warning on one celebrated occasion.

In my early years in politics, Fianna Fáil meetings in Clane, Co. Kildare, took place in Billy King's Hall — known as King's Hall, but not for the usual reasons. I was well into my speech to the party faithful when my voice started to go. Nothing too unusual about that, but in less than thirty seconds, not a sound, not even a whisper which one can usually manage with laryngitis.

Apart from the embarrassment, I nearly passed out with fright, left the meeting immediately, and went home.

Recently, I met an old friend who recalled the incident and regaled the company with 'That was the only time I knew Charlie McCreevy to be stuck for words!'

# SISTER MARGARET MACCURTAIN O.P.

Embarrassment, shyness, being overwhelmed by shame, are three quite different emotions. An embarrassing situation can actually be quite hilarious and I believe the chemistry that turns an embarrassing moment into an episode of merriment and humour is the bond of sympathy that develops between the onlooker and the hapless sufferer of the embarrassment experienced.

Many years ago, when nuns were swathed in long habits and enormous head-dresses, they moved quietly along the streets with their eyes cast down. People tried not to bump into them and workmen on the streets often assisted them chivalrously over flooded water-channels. I was such a young sister, walking swiftly along a city street in my flowing garments, when suddenly a capricious gust of wind blew my large head-dress and veil off into the middle of the road. I was left wearing a neat little white 'bandage' that covered my neck and head and buttoned at the top of my crown (probably from a pattern a thousand years old). For all the world I looked like an Egyptian mummy. My head-dress and veil rolled along the middle of the street, impossible to catch up with, even though I was sprinting hotfoot after it. Then, horrors, a bus hove in sight and it seemed certain that this peculiar large package, my battered head-dress, would be crushed beneath it. About ten people rushed out, waved excitedly to the bus to stop, and endeavoured to catch it. Teasingly, the wind lifted it and bore it like a kite sailing over the bus and landed it on a barber's shop sign where it flapped like a sail in a high wind. Headless and feeling like a hard-boiled egg stripped of its shell, I gazed at it helplessly. Then I was seized with mirth, and all of a sudden everyone was laughing, bus driver, passengers, my would-be rescuers, and the two barbers who had come outside to see what had caused the traffic jam.

In due course, I retrieved a deflated and sodden head-dress. I put it back on my head with a show of composure, only to break into laughter when I caught sight of myself in a shop window, looking like a broken umbrella. A kind woman offered me a lift in her car to the convent, and I departed smiling. Yes, I was embarrassed, but I also realised that for one moment that day people on that street forgot their cares and laughed indulgently at the spectacle of the wind playing games with a young nun in a medieval head-dress.

# JOHN MacKENNA

I can't deny it — I love a practical joke and I've gone to great lengths over the years to catch people out. But when I got caught, it was in a *big* way.

In my work as a radio producer, I get strange letters and requests from time to time. A couple of years ago, I got a letter from a woman who was enquiring about a religious programme I'd produced. I sent back the information and thought nothing more of it. A week later I got another letter from the same woman, outlining a troubled history and asking for advice. I'm no counsellor, but I gave whatever advice I could and directed her to some areas where she might find help.

A fortnight later I got another letter from this woman, much more personal and outlining lots of areas in which she felt she might contribute to radio programmes. Before I had time to reply another letter arrived, even more personal and with a detailed history of a failed marriage. Each letter was followed by another.

As the letters came, I built up a picture of a strange person with strange attitudes — and someone I thought it best to steer clear of! But there was no escape.

Two months after the first letter arrived, the woman called to the radio centre in Donnybrook — with a present for me, a book of religious reflections. But she wasn't as I'd imagined. She was very young, stunningly beautiful, dressed very attractively, outgoing, vivacious . . . overpowering. I talked to her and she left.

Two days later came a letter which said she was in the process of getting her broken marriage together again and, a week later, another letter telling of a successful reconciliation, thanking me for my help (What help? I thought) and telling me her husband and herself planned to call their first baby boy after me!

To be honest, I breathed a sigh of relief. I reckoned I'd had an encounter with a very strange person and got away unscathed. Or so I thought! I told my colleagues about the affair and they were sympathetic and full of advice on what I ought and ought not to have said or done.

And that was that.

A month passed. It was high summer. A colleague invited me to lunch in her house and I agreed to go. She told me there'd be a few other colleagues there, just to celebrate the summer. Fine, I said, sounds lovely.

On the day I turned up at the appointed time. My boss was there and some colleagues and my boss's boss. Nothing too unusual, a dozen people gathered for a nice meal. We sat down and began the lunch. Everything went smoothly and then the dining-room door opened and a latecomer was ushered in, a woman, looking vaguely familiar. She sat opposite me. I knew her but couldn't place her, and then . . . I recognised her . . . the woman who'd written the letters, who'd called to work.

But nobody said anything.

I felt hot, hotter, very hot. What was going on? Then my hostess called for silence and produced a bundle of photocopies of the letters I'd been sent by this strange woman — an actress friend of hers, it turned out — and the woman read the letters to complete my embarrassment but to the delight of the assembled multitude, who had all been in on the four month-long build-up to landing me in it! Lots of helpful comments, hoots, laughter, snide remarks . . . a pool of perspiration on my back.

All I could do was sit there and take it; but I will return . . . watch out, Ruth. I will return. And when I do . . .

# DES MAGUIRE

*Mea Maxima Culpa*

L ong before it was trendy for priests to be trendy, we had a very trendy churchman in a certain rural town in County Kildare. He had passed the seventy mark by the time I got to know him well, but even then he had the heart and mind of an 18-year old, and it was the company of 18-year olds that he craved and sought out, rather than that of his fellow senior citizens. While many of his Maynooth-educated contemporaries still led vigilante committees down rural roads on Friday nights to put the run on courting couples who didn't wait for the last dance in the local hall, Father Bill was cut from a completely different kind of cloth.

He believed that idle teenagers were likely to become dangerous teenagers and that it was far better to have them productively occupied in the pursuits they enjoyed most, rather than roaming all over the place posing a potential threat to themselves and to their fellow man.

So he organised a series of church-backed socials in the parish hall himself on Friday nights and approached a number of the older fellows with driving licences — in those days there was no such thing as a driving test — to bring the teenagers of the parish who had no transport to and from these dances in his own car. Because there were very few cars around in those days, and no driving schools at all, it was a great honour to be appointed one of Fr Bill's 'taxi drivers' and to get the chance to polish up driving skills which would never have stood up to the kind of scrutiny that today's driving inspectors demand.

I thought all my Christmases had come together the day that Fr Bill asked me to become one of his taxi drivers and nodded vigorously in agreement with him as he explained what a huge responsibility he was placing on my shoulders — entrusting other people's lives to me, as well as his own beloved car.

Being one of Fr Bill's taxi drivers gave you a certain status in our community. It meant you had his official seal of approval, that he considered you to be a decent sort of bloke, that you knew the difference between right and wrong.

And once you got that quality mark, like the dog with a good name, you could do no wrong in the eyes of the good people of the town. Nor did I do anything wrong for a long, long time.

When it was my Friday night to pick up or drop people home, not a bottle of beer passed my lips, the car and passengers were collected and left home on time and the keys of the car were always returned safely and on time to Fr Bill. I was definitely a 'sound' man in the parish — one of the soundest around — and the driving was definitely improving with all the practice.

But then, one Friday night, Fr Bill wasn't at home to take safe receipt of either his car or his keys. I waited and waited, but there was no sign of Fr Bill. One o'clock came, two, then three, and still there wasn't a trace or sign of the great man.

Shag this for a lark, I said to myself. I'll go home and return the car in the morning. There's no point leaving it around here to be stolen.

But on my way to Fr Bill's later on that day to deliver the vehicle, a terrible thought struck me. I had completely overlooked a vital piece of information before driving home the night before. Saturday morning was confession morning in our town, and if I needed to make contact with Fr Bill before lunchtime, I had no option but to make that contact in the confessional.

I parked the car close to the church and joined the people queuing up for confession. I said my prayers, moved progressively along the seat closer to the confession box, as each vacancy arose, and gave every appearance of being in the church for the same reason as everybody else.

But when my turn came to confess my sins, I explained to Fr Bill in the secrecy of the confession that I had merely come to deliver his car keys and to tell him where I had left his car. 'I'm sorry about last night,' he said. 'I had to go off to an accident with Dr Tony and had no way of leaving a message for you.'

I explained that I didn't want to leave the car outside his house in case it might be stolen, and he nodded understandingly. We exchanged some further small talk and I left the confession box in the traditional mode, tiptoeing self-consciously like any reformed sinner after firmly resolving to go off and sin no more. I didn't bother to kneel down to say my penance and prayers of contrition, however, as I wanted to move on as quickly as possible, but I could see that this development was attracting quite a deal of attention from the people close to the confession box, all of whom would have known me well from the time I ran around the town in rompers.

'Psst', a neighbour hissed vigorously, offering to shuffle up in her seat and make room so I could finish off my prayers in comfort beside her. 'Psst.'

I kept my head down, making for the door of the church, all the time aware that scores of eyes were burning into the back of my neck.

Then — along with nearly everyone else around — I heard these words which shattered the silence of the church and which I can even hear in my ears, years afterwards, today.

'Where did you say you left the car, lad?'

I turned around, and there was Fr Bill with his head

sticking out of the confession box shouting after me.

Beside me, I could see expressions of deep shock registering on the faces of neighbours who had considered me to be a 'sound' man up to then.

Instead of answering Fr Bill and trying to explain the whole story to very curious neighbours in the middle of the church, I turned around again and made for the door, hoping that the ground would open up and swallow me along the way.

The following day being Sunday meant that Fr Bill had the opportunity of restoring my reputation among the good people of County Kildare from the pulpit, which he did, after we had talked the matter over at some length.

But just as you can give a dog a good name, you can also give him a bad one.

Somehow, right or wrong, I always had the feeling that I was never again regarded as quite so 'sound' by the people of our town after that particular confession.

# BERNIE MALONE

*A Cead Mile Fáilte for a Euro Usher*

It's hard to believe that it's over two years now since I was elected to the European Parliament in Strasbourg. It's an interesting life and I enjoy the work very much. But it does have its embarrassing moments, especially when you're new to the job!

One of my main functions is Vice-President of the Foreign Affairs Committee, where I get the opportunity to greet the heads of state of many countries to the parliament and to chair Question Time with them.

Shortly after my election I was called upon, in that capacity, to chair a special meeting of the committee which was to be addressed by the President of the Ukrainian Parliament, Mr Moroz.

I was in my seat at the top table when the President entered the room, surrounded by a sea of TV cameras, attendant staff, security aides and many others. Shortly before he arrived, the committee's secretariat handed me the President's curriculum vitae for information purposes. However, there was no photograph of him in the file.

When the visiting dignitary arrived, I duly stood up and warmly shook his hand at some length. 'Mr President,' I declared with a broad smile, 'it gives me great pleasure to welcome you to the European Parliament in Strasbourg.' I thought I was doing my very best to put our special guest at his ease.

However, the 'guest' was not at all pleased and quickly pulled his hand away. Imagine my discomfort when he conveyed to me in Spanish that he was not in fact President Moroz, but one of our own ushers who had arrived to prepare the seat next to me for the real President Moroz!

Luckily, no one seemed to notice my mistake and we proceeded to have a very useful discussion about the possibility of closing the Chernobyl nuclear station.

Since then, I assure you, I take a little more care about identifying guests of the parliament when they arrive before I extend my cead mile fáilte.

# MARTIN MANSERGH

As my daughter Alice says, most of us could write an encyclopedia of embarrassing moments. Here are a few entries from mine.

I will always remember the day in October 1967 I first met my future wife Elizabeth at a German Society reading of a play by Brecht in Pembroke College, Oxford. She was a modern languages student from Lady Margaret Hall, and I had rashly vowed I would never marry anyone from my mother's old college. Plucking up the courage to say a few words to this beautiful, unattached student as we came out of Pembroke College, where my father on modest means had come from Ireland to study forty years earlier, I invited her to tea in my rooms across the road in Christ Church. After walking through quad and cloisters and climbing four flights of stairs to the top of the Meadows Building, which looks out on one side to the dreaming spires of Oxford and on the other to the leafy walks of Christ Church Meadow and grazing cattle, I discovered to my embarrassment that I had left my keys locked inside my room. There was nothing for it but to make my excuses to my new friend and leave her standing on the landing, while I hared off to the porter's lodge under the tower of Big Tom to get myself a spare key, and then, a few minutes later, having run the fastest race in my life, tried to appear unruffled as I reached the top of the stairs again.

Liz, who was chatting calmly to my next door neighbour when I returned, thus got a good first impression of my efficiency in practical matters, though she was impressed to find a male student that kept a fruit cake in his room. I wrote in a diary that I kept at the time: 'I met the most fabulous girl today.'

Christ Church in the 1960s was in a state of transition. There was still a small upper crust of aristocrats, but the bulk of students were middle class. The portraits in the dining hall seemed embarrassingly full of eighteenth-century archbishops of the Church of Ireland, lord lieutenants of Ireland, and prime ministers. I still admire Bishop Berkeley of Cloyne, whose philosophy I was studying and who is buried in Christ Church Cathedral (there is a magnificent recumbent effigy in Cloyne), Lewis Carroll for his *Alice* books as well as his mathematical logic, and of course, to a degree, Gladstone, whose portrait used to hang in the family solicitor's in Tipperary town (in contrast to being etched at the bottom of the chamberpot in the Earl of Enniskillen's house in Florence Court).

Another prime minister, Sir Robert Peel, educated at

Christ Church I recently discovered, began his political career by purchasing the pocket borough of Cashel, where in the first decade of the nineteenth century five different members of the Pennefeather family took it in turns to be mayor, to the complete exclusion of anyone else. One Alderman Daniel Mansergh was among the small select number of Cashel electors at that time, but he did sign a petition in favour of Catholic emancipation. (See *My Clonmel Scrapbook*, recently republished.) The Lord Lieutenant Wellesley sent down Peel's surname, promising to send on details of the Christian name shortly. The fact that for the price of £1,000 or more Tipperary gave Peel his political start in life did not of course mean he looked kindly on Tipperary. As Chief Secretary and Home Secretary, he responded harshly enough to troubles there, but unlike his successor, Lord John Russell, at least he knew what to do when famine broke out in 1845.

Certain members of Christ Church had an embarrassing habit when drunk late at night, of singing 'Land of Hope and Glory' and 'Rule Britannia' at the top of their voices, and accosting unfortunate passers-by like myself and interrogating them on their loyalty. One of them, a member of a ruling family since the days of Queen Elizabeth, as in a certain famous Russian novel, liked to stand on the ledge of his first-floor window in the Peckwater Quad and lean over backwards to down a vodka. One evening, unfortunately, he fell to the ground. While surviving that escapade, he went to fight as a volunteer for Ian Smith in Rhodesia and was killed doing so. Another fellow student, a pleasant double-barrelled son of well-to-do Catholic gentry in County Kildare, tried to do his finals politics revision from W. H. Smith 'O' level revision cards. His family some years ago went out of the mushroom business. I am not surprised that another student at the time, one Bill Clinton, was not entirely impressed, especially as the upper classes in England still tended at that time to look down on Americans as parvenus. One of my tutors whom I respected seemed to prefer from his students an appreciation of wine (he was after all the custodian of the college wine cellar) to zeal in philosophical studies, and he once suggested that I might need a brain transplant if I were to get a first. But my politics and economics tutors were subsequently two of the three key organisers of the successful campaign to deny Margaret Thatcher an honorary doctorate at Oxford University in 1984.

I had a picture in my mind of the Tom Quadrangle at Christ Church, when Peter Brooke told the British-Irish Association a story to illustrate his trials as Northern Secretary trying to organise all-party talks. An intoxicated don was discovered wandering around naked, much to the embarrassment of a college porter, late at night, who asked him if he needed any assistance. The don declined, saying that the quad was spinning about him, but when he saw his doorway come round he would make a dash for it!

I remember going in 1973 to a public meeting in City Hall addressed by the Tory Chancellor of the Exchequer, and asking a critical question about the inflationary consequences of their expansionary policies, and being disgusted by the put-down of a reply I received, which was: 'You did not get much applause for that question.'

To revert to family: Liz and I first had two daughters, but my parents were very keen to have a grandson, the family name being fairly thin on the ground. At this stage I had joined the Department of Foreign Affairs and had been posted to Bonn. I was so excited, when Daniel was born in Bonn in December 1976 in the Johanniter Krankenhaus (it took him some time as a child to accept that this did not make him German), that I crashed the car into pillars underneath the embassy as I went back to celebrate. Some of my daughters have complained since, why I did not crash the car on the occasion of their birth! When I unpopped a champagne cork in the embassy upstairs, it narrowly missed the late Ambassador Robin Fogarty, who protested he was getting too old for that sort of thing. When I rang home to

Tipperary (it was just before Christmas), my mother ran to my father and informed him: 'Daniel Mansergh has arrived.' He immediately assumed that this was yet another distant relative turning up on the doorstep from California or Australia. Older Germans looked a little surprised at the choice of Daniel as a name, and commented, 'That's Jewish, isn't it?' But I had a lonely Christmas on my own with my two daughters, Fiona and Lucy, eating the toughest and most famished turkey from Poland that I have ever had in my life (in contrast to the succulent Silver Hill duckling that we served our German guests at dinner parties). Mind you, I will always remember when our fifth child Harriet was born in Holles Street in 1985, Ned O'Keeffe predicting to me in Leinster House: 'Begob, Martin, you will be needing a bigger pocket now.'

I had my first real experience of negotiation in Bonn. Being the most junior member of the embassy in those days meant being charged with, among other things, 'unimportant' diplomatic tasks, like finding a larger embassy building and negotiating the lease (subject to ultimate departmental approval, of course). I had some experience in cattle markets, and I felt I had talked down the rent quite satisfactorily from the original price. Everything seemed tied up, when suddenly, to my intense embarrassment, the developers put in a last-minute demand for a monthly rental per parking space of DM 120, compared with the DM 47 that we were paying at our existing building and the DM 60 I had expected. I was so incensed that, taking a leaf out of the negotiating style of Robin Fogarty (my Ambassador), I created a scene, and said that we would not pay more than half that sum, and no way would we move in on such terms. To my chagrin, when I recounted this to him, the Ambassador was not one bit pleased, saying that we had to have an embassy, and we needed parking spaces. Fortunately, the Dutch property company came back the next day and agreed to the DM 60 figure, saving me sooner or later from being reduced to making an undignified retreat from too exposed and unsupported a position. While an Office of Public Works official out there expressed some appreciation, he knew as well as I did that you do not necessarily get any thanks for saving money in the civil service, and the only reward would be a sense of personal satisfaction. The Embassy will, I suppose, be shortly moving on to Berlin.

President Hillery came on a state visit to Bonn in 1977, accompanied by the Minister for Foreign Affairs, Dr Garret FitzGerald and his wife Joan. I remember being sent on a wild goose chase by my colleague Joe Hayes, Garret's former private secretary, after one of Joan's coats, on the grounds that it might have been mislaid on a train. A fellow Tipperary man from Thurles, he was enormous fun, capable of creating a drama out of the smallest incident of everyday life.

One morning, when the presidential party was about to check out of an inn in Bavaria, once slept in by the Empress Maria Theresa of Austria, there was an SOS from Dr FitzGerald. The Minister had rejoined the party from a late-night Brussels ministerial meeting, arriving at the inn at about 5 a.m. There was a Germanic-style notice on all the doors, saying that luggage was to be left outside the door by 7 a.m. So he quickly undressed and put the suitcase quietly outside the door so as not to disturb his wife. Unfortunately, he had also packed the socks he was wearing. So when I arrived at his room at the top of the stairs, Dr FitzGerald opened the door and started waggling his bare toes at me, asking could I get him a pair of socks. The innkeeper duly sent me back with two pairs, which earned me the ministerial commendation of a 'most efficient service'.

Finally, of course, there is political embarrassment. (There are some members of the public who claim to find all politics embarrassing.) I remember being seated next to Charles Haughey, and metaphorically fastening the seat belt at a couple of turbulent press conferences after the Anglo-Irish Summit of November 1981 and the publication of the

Forum Report in May 1984, as a large, agitated and excited posse of journalists fired hostile questions at the table. P. J. Mara has recounted many times the seismic impact of the famous *Hot Press* interview on the fifth floor of Leinster House. There were also occasions when, after speeches Haughey had worked hard at and considered important did not get the full press coverage he felt they deserved, he would look hard at the unfortunate Mara and ask witheringly: 'Why do we bother putting so much work into our speeches?' P. J. and I worked exceptionally well together, without friction; but I remember one day in Government Buildings ringing him early in the morning to seek clarification of some item in the press. To my surprise, he starting hectoring and shouting down the phone at me, and treating my questions as very stupid, in the colourful way that I sometimes heard him put down obtuse young reporters with a tiresome line of enquiry. When he put down the phone, he called out to his clerical assistant: 'Sinead, who was that?' When he found out, he came running into my office, next door along the corridor, apologising and laughing profusely.

Marx once said that history repeats itself, first as tragedy then as farce. On our way back from Australia, in the autumn of 1994, Albert Reynolds as Taoiseach was due to meet President Yeltsin in Dromoland on the Shannon stopover, on the model of Charles Haughey's meeting with President Gorbachev in March 1990, a great but ultimately tragic figure. The Taoiseach Albert Reynolds and his ministers stood patiently on the tarmac as Yeltsin failed to appear. Gradually, as time passed, one could sense mounting excitement among the waiting press corps, that there might be a real story in the offing, instead of the usual tedious co-operation protocols and official photocalls. Albert took it all in very good part and saw the funny side, and if his dignity was offended he did not show it. In political terms, the incident, coupled with one or two others of a similar kind, as when he seized the baton from the conductor of a brass band in Germany, caused more embarrassment to President Yeltsin or, perhaps more accurately, his colleagues.

# MAXI

'Tell her to get down,' I hissed, wondering who the person was passing by, but trusting they'd do as I said. No one moved. 'Tell her it's unprofessional to be sitting up there in costume,' I added. No one moved.

The scene took place in Castlebar General Hospital. The source of my troubles, the image of Marion Fossett, long dark hair framing her face, sitting in an alcove in the wall, high above us all.

I was getting angrier now: Marion Fossett, Frances Campbell and myself had sung for Ireland in Eurovision this year, 1981, as Sheeba. We had been working constantly ever since. Europe we had taken by storm, and Tokyo was waiting to welcome us in just three weeks. After that we had a fifteen week series on Thames Television. Ahead of all that, I had to get Marion down from the alcove before any of the press spotted her, or before we knew it we'd have something to explain in the papers.

'Get her down from there,' I screamed at the first passer-by. This time a kindly nun calmed me with her sweet soft words. 'Time you rested, Max,' she purred in my ear. 'Everything will be fine if you calm down a little.'

'Are you going to the reception?' says I. 'Time you weren't here. They are all in there you know. Come on, I'll introduce you.'

We walked together into the main reception room. 'There's Fred O'Donovan, my mum, my dad, Brendan Grace, Karen Black, Roy Taylor, Herta Fossett, Mick Quinn, Peter Dempsey . . .'

I was using my best voice, taught in school, St Louis, and

I knew they'd be proud of my projection.

'A little more rest,' said the nun, 'and you'll be so much better.'

'How can I rest?' I argued, 'some of these people are meeting for the first time. I have to circulate.'

'Yes, dear,' she sighed.

'And, Jesus Mary and Joseph, get Fossett down from that wall . . .'

It was the voices of my mum and dad that finally cracked into my subconscious.

Slowly, clearly, they repeated again and again that I had been in a car crash. There had been two fatalities, a young mother and her child. We had been on our way to Castlebar to set keys of songs for our new album to be recorded in Hilversum, Holland, later that month. The Dutch song-writers were there for a week's fishing and thought they'd mix biz and pleasure.

On the way down we had crashed. Frances was in intensive care with a collapsed lung. Marion had also got no further than intensive care, as she had multiple lacerations on her face and was on the bed opposite me, with bandages, it appears, just about everywhere.

I, on the other hand, had jolted to the roof of the car on impact. Because the roof was torn, it had cut my head. Rushed into hospital, I had gone into a coma for several days; when I woke I wasn't making any sense at all.

Being carefully monitored by experts on head injuries, they noted that when I did finally wake up, I had remembered the faces and voices of those I had recently met, but had put them in the most unusual circumstances in my damaged brain.

Embarrassing? You betcha.

Time passed, and Frances went home. A little later, Marion was moved to Dublin for further facial surgery.

Alone in Castlebar, Co. Mayo, the county of my mother's birth, I rested and slowly recovered enough to accept the offer of a lift home with mam, dad and my brother Brendan.

The kindly nun was there to see me off.

Just before I set off, she reminded me how lucky I had been. It couldn't have been said enough times, as my memory needed all the help it could get to restore 100 per cent working ability.

'I'm so embarrassed,' I confided to her, as I pulled my warm clothes tightly around me, preparing for the journey, 'mouthing off like that, disturbing all the other patients, and where did I get the idea about Marion hanging out, in the wall?'

The nun led me gently back up the corridor. We stopped at the door to intensive care and she unlocked it. There was no one ill in the room, so I had a moment to take in the details.

The bed I had previously occupied really did face an alcove in the wall. In it, a life-size statue of the Sacred Heart.

# KEVIN MORAN

In normal life, embarrassing moments pass quickly and silently. Not so on a football pitch in front of thousands of people!

Although I can recall several incidents in my playing career that have embarrassed me, I will tell you the following story.

In the winter of '82, I noticed that my eyesight was not as spot on as it had been. Reading small print was more difficult now, and so I took myself off to an optician. As a youngish man, I wasn't too keen to wear glasses, particularly on the pitch, and given that the lads in the dressing room need only a small excuse to start the slagging! Therefore, I opted for a pair of contact lenses which were easy to wear and forget about.

Soon after that, during a match, Justin Fashanu and I went up for a ball at the same time, and boom! Collision.

I remember falling to the ground with a thud and when I opened my eyes I felt all woozy and dazed, so I just lay there. Gordon McQueen, Arthur Albiston and Gary Bailey all crowded around me to see if I was OK.

'I can't see. It's all hazy', said yours truly, and so the medics were called on to the pitch. After a brief examination of my head and eyes, they decided I must be concussed and should be taken off. I didn't feel bad, but didn't protest because not being able to see was starting to worry me, just a bit!

The substitute appeared at the sideline ready to run on in my place, and Gordon and Arthur gently helped me up while Justin apologised for making such hard contact with me. Contact! It suddenly clicked that instead of being concussed I may simply have lost my lenses, and with that, I dropped quickly to the ground again and started scrabbling around, patting the grass where I had fallen. I am sure for a second or so the others thought that I had really lost it before I explained. Gordon, Arthur, Gary and Justin then all dropped to the ground to help me look. Totally forgetting that we were being watched by thousands of fans, we crawled around on our hands and knees, parting blades of grass. I am sure the unfolding drama had everyone gripped — what on earth were we doing?

The penny must have dropped because I heard a snigger or two from the watching crowd. How could I have confused losing a contact lens with concussion? After a few more minutes, more of us were scrabbling around on the ground, surrounded by bemused medics, team mates and a stadium full of fans. We gave up. Head down, I ambled back into position as nonchalantly as possible, given the sarcastic clapping, to allow the game to continue.

Needless to say, I kept well in the background for the remainder of the game.

# PADDY MURRAY

We were having a grand day in Powerscourt. We were on a hike with the Blackrock College boy scout troop. And like all boy scouts, we had to do everything the hard way. Not for us the simple method of crossing the River Dargle. We wouldn't be using the bridge. We'd build one ourselves.

And so we decided to sling a rope from one tree to another on the far bank of the river.

Naturally, I was the one designated to climb the tree and secure the rope. It was a job I undertook successfully. Until . . . I heard a cracking sound, a branch broke, and I fell twenty feet, landing on the base of my spine. There was much laughter, no sympathy — and a five mile walk back to the bus stop.

By the time I got home I was in agony.

And so it was decided that I would be brought to St Vincent's Hospital, the old one in St Stephen's Green, the following day. My father brought me in and we were about to queue for the X-ray department, when he met a doctor friend of his who said we could skip the queue and have the X-ray done privately.

So I was marched into a room where I was greeted by a vision. She was beautiful. I was about 13 in the first stirrings of youth. She was in her early twenties, blonde, slim, gorgeous.

A few years earlier I wouldn't have noticed. But girls were now firmly on the agenda.

She shook my hand and told me to go into a cubicle, undress and put on the gown that was hanging there. I was mortified. But the back was sore and there was nothing to do but follow instructions.

I undressed. I put on the gown and walked out of the cubicle.

'Lie up on the table,' she said. And I did. 'Now, open the gown,' she said.

Oh, my God! Open the gown! It was, I thought, my worst nightmare. But it was only just beginning. I closed my eyes and opened the gown. Then I looked at her. And she had one of those smiles on her face that indicated she was pitying me.

'Ah,' she said. 'You could have kept your underpants on.'

# P. J. NOLAN

*Farming Olympics*

There's no time like the present, says I.

I woke up the other morning and headed off to get the cows in. It was so frosty that I had to tell Mutlet two shaggy dog stories to coax him out of his shed. It was foggy, too, so we went on a cow-searching odyssey.

Then I began to dream. 1996, of course, is Olympic year with fifty of our most talented athletes having done their best against the world.

First I picked up a big stone, threw it and hurt my shoulder, so that ruled me out of the shot putt. Next I ran across the field after cow number 431 and she got away, even though she's lame — so that ruled me out of the 10,000 metres.

I jumped the ditch and fell back in, losing a welly, so that left me out of the long jump. Even if I did go, sure I'd be done for drugs because I have progesterone and oestradiol to try and get the cows in calf, not to mention stomach boluses and baytril for calves, so the international jury wouldn't be too happy with me.

Bicycle racing is out because I know I'm no good at that.

That only leaves fencing, but with a bad hammer and cheap three inch wire and crooked staples, I'd probably fail in the qualifying rounds. So at a quarter to seven in a badly reseeded field, I realised I'd never win the Olympics unless we got a farming Olympics.

I wonder now!

We could have a rugby tournament. Of course, the New Zealanders would be odds on to win that from the Australians (the average Irish farmer is too slow to compete). The paper-chase, on the other hand, is a different kettle of fish.

What with all the maps, subsidy forms and declarations, the Irish farmer would be odds on to qualify for the final eight.

As self-appointed manager of the Irish Farm Olympics team, I've decided to nominate Minister Yates for the juggling team, because he is the only man in history to keep eight balls in the air for three weeks without letting them all fall. Mind you, present difficulties might render him unavailable for selection, especially if there's any chance of intervention by a third party.

The favourites for the porridge-making competition are the English pair of Steven Dorrell and Douglas Hogg, because over the past while they've shown that they can make a complete hash out of anything they put their minds to.

Seeing as it's a farming Olympics, I want to have a motorised section in the race-against-the-clock section. I'm nominating the milk tanker drivers of Ireland who can get an eight foot wide truck through a seven foot gate and can negotiate double parked cars outside a country chapel on a Sunday morning, not to mention reversing blind round three corners with new flower beds on either side.

So, with this experience, the lorry-driving section of the farmer Olympics should be chickenfeed. Oops, there's another dirty word.

Sheep shearing, cow milking and turkey plucking are all marvellous spectator sports, unless of course you're bovine, ovine or avian, in which case you could end up being shorn, plucked or squeezed, or all three if you were really unlucky!

# DAVID NORRIS

As far as embarrassment is concerned, I could I suppose be said to suffer from an *embarras de richesse*. Since a young age I have shown an innate talent in propelling myself into situations which cause embarrassment both to myself and others. Some of these incidents are, I think, fairly widespread and in general I am sure many people have shared exactly the same situation. For example, when very tiny I remember being taken into town by my mother when she went shopping in Brown Thomas's shop in Grafton Street. Either I wandered away or my mother drifted off some yards from the counter from where she had originally been stationed. I got bored, spotted my mother's dress, decided it was time to go, punched her firmly on the backside, pulled the hem of her skirt and said, 'Let's go home now.' I was rewarded by the sight of a considerably puzzled middle-aged matron wearing similar clothes to my mother turning round and saying, 'What is wrong little boy?'

An even worse occasion occurred during a children's party at a friend's house. Having consumed the usual vast quantities of lemonade, I made my way up the stairs, opened the lavatory door, disclosing my friend's father seated on the pot reading the newspaper. He slammed the door shut with a quick movement of his foot shouting, 'Get out of here.' Children's parties were fertile grounds for embarrassment. On another occasion I was attempting to sink my teeth into a well-filled cream bun. As a result of my efforts a large glob of cream was ejaculated from the side of the bun right on to the drawing-room carpet as the host's mother advanced to say hello. To spare myself from the awkwardness of the situation, I immediately put my foot on the offending dollop of cream. I realised I had been unsuccessful when, following the gaze of this refined woman, I saw that my little black shoe was now surrounded by a billowing fringe of freshly whipped cream.

Even adulthood and political life have not spared my blushes. Some years ago I went to Australia to take part in a meeting of the Interparliamentary Union. On my way I took in a trip to China flying into Sydney and on to Canberra from Beijing.

I arrived mid-afternoon a bit frayed at the edges and then went out with the rest of the party to the Irish Ambassador's residence. We got back by about nine o'clock, by which time I was so exhausted that without bothering to unpack the pyjamas which I do occasionally wear, I took a quick shower and hit the sheets. It was a luxurious hotel. We each had a commodious suite with a series of interconnecting rooms including a bathroom. At three o'clock in the morning I woke up and got out of bed to go to the lavatory. I had my eyes half closed, pushed open the lavatory door and heard it close gently but firmly behind me. Opening my eyes fully, I discovered to my horror that I was now out in the lobby of the hotel stark ballocked naked with no means of getting back into my room. This posed something of a problem. In the suite next door was a distinguished political colleague and his wife. Should I ring the bell? If I did, and with my reputation for advanced thinking in sexual matters, my appearance completely naked at three o'clock in the morning might be misconstrued. The solution I eventually found was to whip a pair of cushions from a sofa thoughtfully placed in the vestibule and apply one fore and one aft to make my way to the reception desk, where my sudden materialisation in a state of undress jolted the staff from their late night reverie. I am glad to say that they believed my story, provided me with a pass key and let me resume my interrupted slumber.

# ARNOLD J. O'BYRNE

**M**ost embarrassing moments generally, with hindsight, have a humorous side to them. It is, unfortunately, only later and often much, much later that one can laugh at them.

One such embarrassing occurrence happened to me when I worked in London.

It was Ash Wednesday, 1959, and I was working in Fleet Street. I was, in fact, a finance clerk in Reuters, the news agency. However, I believed then that the simple statement of 'working in Fleet Street' had a more exciting ring to it than just saying I was a finance clerk.

At that time, and I have no reason to believe it has changed, the nearest Roman Catholic church was located in High Holborn, just a short walk from Fleet Street. It was called St Ethelredas.

As it was Ash Wednesday, I decided to go along to lunchtime Mass, myself and many others.

When I arrived at the church it was packed to almost overflowing. It was standing room only, shoulder to shoulder, and then only at the back of the church. Not to be deterred, I fought my way to the back, found my standing space and joined in the Mass.

A finance clerk was not a highly paid position; in truth, it was not even an average paid position. However, from my wages I had somehow managed to save enough money to buy a raincoat.

The coat was what one would call a trench coat. It was military in style and fawn in colour and, in my opinion, added to the image of one 'working in Fleet Street'.

It was fashionable to wear the coat unbelted. The belt hung loosely at the back with the ends pushed into the appropriate side pockets. For added effect the collar was turned up, regardless of the weather.

As I stood there, deep in prayer, I was aware of being

enveloped by a great warmth. I was, I assumed, being filled by the Holy Spirit with tongues of fire.

Fire! That one word brought me in double quick time from my heavenly plane to the more realistic earthly plane. 'Fire! You're on fire!' the surrounding congregation shouted, as they scattered away from me.

I was reminded of the parable of the leper ringing the bell and shouting 'unclean' so that people would not come near him. Whilst I had no bell, the word 'fire' seemed as effective as 'unclean'.

The feeling of contented warmth had now changed to uncomfortable heat. My pride and joy, my military-style trench coat, my image builder, was on fire and, even worse, I was still wearing it.

The loosely hanging belt had been ignited by a candle some petitioner had lit in front of a statue. Probably a statue to St Blaize!

The word 'quickly' would be inappropriate to describe the speed with which I whipped off my coat, rolled it up and extinguished the flames.

Slowly and with what I hope was an air of nonchalance for one 'working in Fleet Street', I unrolled my treasure to discover the back completely burned. In fact, where the back had been was just one big hole.

I shed many silent tears.

I stood for the remainder of the Mass, far removed from the offending candle, in a daze, wondering how I was going to replace my coat, my image builder.

The priest distributed the ashes intoning as he did so, 'Ashes to ashes, dust to dust.' I silently added the words, 'To buy a new raincoat is now a must.'

As the Mass drew to an end, the priest turned to the congregation and said: '*Ite, Missa est*' (Go, the Mass is ended). Never I am sure in the history of the Mass has anybody responded with as much sincerity as I when I said: '*Deo gratias*' (Thanks be to God).

It was certainly one Mass, one Ash Wednesday, and one raincoat I will never forget.

# BRENDAN O'CARROLL

*Field of Screams*

Most people will find it hard to believe that I could ever be embarrassed. Now, I'm not going to play the old comedian and say that I'm a lot more timid or shy than people realise, because that wouldn't be the truth. I certainly have my embarrassing moments, but the lucky thing about being a comedian is that most people don't expect that I'm embarrassed, so a lot of the time it's easy to hide. It would be difficult to pick my most embarrassing moment, but certainly there was one which sticks in my mind probably because it happened on a football field and with team mates. I took a ribbing for it for a long time afterwards.

At the height of my footballing career, if I had one talent it was speed. Over five yards, which is the critical distance in football, there were very few people who could outrun me.

The football match I'm referring to took place on a wet and cold day in a Dublin soccer stadium best left unnamed, and likewise the two teams involved. I was playing double centre forward and they were playing a 'flat back three' which, as football *aficionados* will know, gave me the opportunity to try and outrun their offside trap. In the first half I had beaten the offside trap on three occasions, only to hear when I reached the ball the shrill blast of the referee's whistle. My reaction to these three 'mistakes' by the referee was of, let's say, timid disagreement, although there are a couple of League of Ireland referees, i.e. Pat Kelly and Paddy Daly, who might disagree with that!

It certainly seemed that this referee was not going to give me the benefit of the doubt in any offside situation, so I decided to pull the play back to our half-way line, giving me an opportunity to run on to the ball from within my own half. Within minutes of dragging the play back, my plan worked. Pat Sullivan, probably the most talented midfield player I have ever played with, laid the ball directly at my feet. I was at least three yards inside my own half and with my back to the opponents' goal. I could hear the grunt of the centre-half as he ploughed down towards me from behind. I turned, flicked the ball and 'nutmegged' the centre-half, pushing the ball about five yards into the opposition's half and ran on to it. Just as I reached the ball and tapped it forward well clear, I heard once again the referee's whistle. I glanced to the left-hand side of the field; the linesman stood firmly with his flag by his side. Now I was mad, really mad. I bent down, picked up the ball and slowly turned towards the referee. I threw the ball at him roaring, 'What the fuck are yeh blowin' for now?'

The referee calmly picked up the ball, smiled at me and very quietly said: 'It's half-time, son.'

I left the field, my head bowed to the claps and slagging of my team mates and the crowd. Before we kicked off for the second half, the referee walked up to me and said: 'Brendan, I'm going to blow the whistle now and that means the second half has started. Is that OK?'

Which was met with a roar of laughter by both teams. I even joined in myself.

# MARK O'CONNELL

*An Embarrassing Little Tale*

When I was a little boy, I never asked my parents for much. Money was never exactly in abundance, so invariably I would — to use modern parlance — down-size requests for clothes, toys and sweets.

But at one stage in my childhood — I think I was about 7 years of age — I decided that I wanted to acquire a hearing aid. This was, in my considered view, the ultimate accessory for the kid who wanted to look cool in the 1970s — a sort of male version of an earring.

The only problem I had with this sophisticated device was that my hearing was perfectly fine. Clearly, I would have to feign deafness or at least partial deafness if my great ambition was to be fulfilled.

This was relatively easy to do. I began ignoring things my mother and father would say to me, particularly when they would order me to do my school exercise, clean my bedroom or go to bed. They weren't moved one way or the other. Wouldn't any self-respecting child pretend not to hear such things?

If I was to succeed at all, I realised I would have to turn the deaf ear to them even when they would offer me nice things like more jelly in my dessert or a few shillings to buy myself a Dinky.

This was indeed a more clever tack. Before too long, I overheard them discussing the possibility of me being hard of hearing. I kept it up for a few days more and, sure enough, one day they told me — in louder than usual tones — that they would be taking me to a hospital to see if they could do something to improve my hearing.

I congratulated myself on the nice work.

Off we went one rainy Monday after school to the Eye and Ear Hospital on Adelaide Road. The doctor, a cheerful middle-aged lady with a blue rinse hair-do, looked in my ears with a tiny torch and flushed warm water into both. She then brought me into what looked like a broadcasting studio and placed a set of massive headphones on my head. All sorts of weird sounds were played through the speakers and my facial gestures were being monitored. She later began to talk to me about school, about what subjects I liked, what I wanted to be when I grew up.

But I was wise to her. There was no way I was going to play that game. I gave the ol' deaf ear bit the best shot I could. And as sure as I was putting it on, she turned to my mother and declared that I was 'profoundly deaf'.

My mother, trying to hold back the tears, was told that my problem could be mitigated if — wait for it — I was to wear a hearing aid. My mother went along with the suggestion, albeit reluctantly, and before leaving the hospital I was fitted for my very own hearing aid which would be ready for collection the following week.

An entirely successful operation, I thought. I simply couldn't wait to get it into my ear. I would be the envy of the whole school. On the bus journey home, I asked my inconsolable mother if I would be allowed to wear my hearing aid when we had visitors.

She duly discussed the matter with my father and, before collecting the hearing aid, they thought it best to get a second opinion — just in case. I was duly taken to a magnificent house in Monkstown where one of the city's top ear specialists had his 'rooms'.

This was a different class of medical man entirely. While he carried out the same kind of tests as the lady a few days before, he appeared just a little unconvinced.

'One moment, Mark,' he said to me. 'I want to go outside and have a word with your mother. Just wait there like a good boy.'

I remember the man getting up from his embossed leather-covered desk and walking slowly towards the door. As it opened, my attention was captured by the low swishing sound of the heavy door gliding over the deep-pile carpet.

Looking over his shoulder, the doctor noticed me marvelling at the sound made by the movement of the door. It was all over for my hearing aid. As he continued on out of the room to my mother, I had a sinking feeling.

'That boy's hearing is perfect,' I heard him say very clearly. 'A hearing aid is the last thing he needs, Mrs O'Connell. May I suggest you show him more affection. Perhaps you might treat him to an ice-cream from time to time . . .'

I had a lot of explaining to do. And, needless to say, ice-cream was not on the menu in the O'Connell household for quite a long time afterwards.

# KEVIN O'CONNOR

During the James Joyce Centenary celebrations in 1982, there was a grand gathering in the newly refurbished State Apartments in Dublin Castle, to which 'the great and the good' among the country's artistic community were invited. (Yes, I know, I don't qualify under the heading — there are exceptions to every rule.)

I was in conversation with Pauline Bewick, the artist, when a stern-looking woman came and stood beside us. As Pauline assumed I should know her companion and as I didn't have a clue who she was, I made some floundering efforts to glean her identity, to which she responded with a hostile stare.

Noticing she was sporting a man's tweed hat of the sort worn by tourist fishermen in Connemara — replete with hooks in circular symmetry — I angled (!) for conversation. 'Do you fish?' I asked. The stare became more hostile.

As nobody came to 'fish' me out of that hole and the communal silence lengthened, I made a last desperate throw. 'Ah I know — you're Pauline's mother!'

Hell hath no fury than a woman deemed considerably older than she feels. If looks could kill . . . As the company looked aghast, I shrank away, to be told by Pauline later that her companion was the famous Irish painter XY, and that while she may have appeared to me to be old enough to be Pauline's mother, I was not to be thanked for saying so . . .

# LIZ O'DONNELL

*'Bears Blast Goldilocks'*

Asingle telephone call to New York clinched it. The holiday was sorted. A child-free week in September divided between the Hamptons and New York city was just the ticket for two stressed-out couples. Grandparents and other essential support services were brought on side, tickets booked, diaries notified.

We left the details of house and car rental to my friend, Janet. Like many Irish emigrants, she had prospered in the States, advancing from illegal waitress to catering entre-preneur.

Come September, having urged Janet not to skimp, we were none the less slightly alarmed to hear that a limo would pick us up at Kennedy and drive us the two hours to our rented house at Sag Harbour. Visions of running out of cash after the first two hours of the holiday! The limo turned out to be little more than a minibus and not the black-windowed superstar variety.

Soon the motorway, clogged with unfamiliar vehicles, was replaced by picket fences and wooden houses. Boats tinkled in the harbour. Sag Harbour looked rich. There were no visible signs of crime or poverty. No beggars or litter. American flags fluttered in the balmy September breeze.

The driver had the directions and seemed to know where he was going. We weaved slowly down the leafy avenues which bordered the water's edge. The wooden houses were all different, but of a style with large unstructured gardens, trees with hammocks and verandas with rocking chairs.

We had arrived. To our surprise the house was unlocked. Coming from security-conscious Dublin, we were amazed that the door opened to a push. Inside, the style was Hampton's Habitat: huge open hearth, dried flowers, ethnic pottery, Indian wall hangings. The kitchen too was predictably tasteful. An enormous fridge groaned with wine, beer, salads, patés and cheeses. We cracked open a bottle, kicked off the shoes and settled in.

The lads decided to investigate the garden and go for a dip, leaving a trail of clothing down to the lapping ocean. I called Janet on her mobile. She was catering a wedding and was just finishing up. She would be with us shortly. An hour passed. The lads were slugging beer in their dripping togs. The women were quaffing wine and cheese. The music was blaring. No sign of Janet. I called her again.

'Where are you?' she bellowed.

'What do you mean, where are we? We are here in the house.'

'But,' said Janet, 'I'm in the house and you're not here.'

Pandemonium. We were in the wrong house.

'Get out of there,' shrieked Janet. 'Over here they shoot first and ask questions later.'

Already the house was a mess: empty beer cans, remains of cheese, dirty wine glasses, pools of water from the dripping swimmers, towels strewn about, bags half unpacked. I tried not to think about the appalling vista of the police arriving. 'Yes, officer. I really am an Irish TD.' The tabloid headlines 'Bears blast Goldilocks'. What if shots were fired? My Chappaquidick!

As we hauled out the bags, miraculously, along came Janet. The real house was next door, fifty yards along the bay. She bundled us into her jeep.

Next morning, the two lads swam slowly past the evacuated house. There were signs of movement within. We made no contact. I'm sure they are still wondering what happened that hot afternoon in September.

# GAY O'DRISCOLL

The most embarrassing moment of my life has to be a few years ago when I was asked to get involved in setting up a community centre in O'Devaney Gardens.

The financing of this was difficult and we decided to run a fund-raising night in O'Hanlon's on the North Circular Road and get the community of O'Devaney Gardens involved in selling it. I looked after the entertainment and asked some friends of mine to perform on the night. They included Fr Michael Cleary, Paddy and Kevin Glacken and Sean Potts.

The tickets sold very well and we looked forward to a good evening. The plan was that Fr Michael would get the evening going and have everyone in good form straight away, which he did; then the Glackens and Sean Potts would follow with some lively music and round off with a disco. Everything went according to plan and the evening was a great success both financially and socially. Fr Michael was great, the Glackens and Sean Potts were excellent, and the disco started. I was sitting with Paddy Glacken, Sean Potts and his wife Bernie having a drink, feeling very happy, when one of the female patrons, who had already taken one too many, approached Paddy and asked, 'Are you in de band?' Paddy replied that he was and she said, 'Well, yez were fucking brutal.' I was glad they were particularly good friends and we all had a good laugh, but nevertheless I was most embarrassed. These people have played all around the world to audiences of tens of thousands and here they were, giving their services free as a favour to me.

# ANDY O'MAHONY

The first LP I ever bought was a recording of Beethoven's Fifth Symphony. Not any old version, mind you, but that by Erich Kleiber and the Concertgebouw of Amsterdam. Music lovers of a certain age still talk about that dazzling interpretation. The great conductor's son, Carlos Kleiber, was recently described by Sir Isaiah Berlin as the best conductor working today. The evidence for this is on compact disc, a technology unknown to his father. But the older technology was a more tempting piece of merchandise: LPs looked better. That Beethoven recording came in a grey/white/beige jacket with musical notation in red and black. It was the first piece to be played on my new Black Box, the most compact unit of all time. It must be forty years ago. The Bank of Ireland had assigned me to its Listowel branch at the beginning of November. Music was a solace in the long winter evenings. As were amateur theatricals. On the strength of owning the Beethoven Fifth, I was offered a leading part in M. J. Molloy's *The Will and the Way*.

In one of Mr Molloy's less subtle moments, the hero says, 'And thus Fate comes knocking at the door', followed by the opening chords of Beethoven's Fifth. The problem was that in addition to saying the line, I had to operate a record player on stage. None of your offstage musical effects in those days. Still, it sounded straightforward enough. So, I uttered the words, moved upstage and dropped the arm on the turntable. Let me add two further vital pieces of information: new record players are notoriously unpredictable; and my own psychomotor skills leave a lot to be desired. That unhappy conjunction led to a moment of theatre unintended by either the playwright or the producer, the late Brendan Carroll. I must have tried the operation at least four times. The first failure might have been interpreted generously as due to a change of mind on the part of the character on stage, who had suddenly decided that instead of listening to Beethoven he was going to go for a walk. The second failure presented a bigger challenge to the tolerance of the audience. Still, perhaps the two mishaps could be seen as part of a complex web of character development. But that was my last chance. Not a sound from the record player. Not even a click. Had the infernal machine exploded, I would have been saved. Nothing prepares you for the humiliation of silence.

What happened next on stage has been excised from my memory. Afterwards, there were mutterings about faulty equipment and the need for rehearsal, a concept then in its infancy in the amateur theatre. There was a suggestion that I should have hummed the opening bars. It was many years later that I heard about the South American tenor who stopped just before 'Di quella pira' in *Trovatore* and announced that, by special request, he was going to sing 'Come Back to Sorrento' instead. That's the way to do it. All I remember is taking off my make-up and going back on stage to retrieve that Kleiber recording of the Beethoven Fifth. The stained honey-colour cabinet of the offending record player remains forever part of my colour-map. I dusted off the record, put it back in its grey/white/beige cover, and walked home in the dark. Yes, it must be forty years ago.

# BRENDAN O'REILLY

Regular appearances on TV inevitably ensure a share of embarrassing moments and this was especially true in the early days of RTE TV when inexperience was frequently 'thrown in at the deep end'. Like the occasion on 'Sports Final', when I was given what I thought was a late 'sports flash'. As I reached out for the sheet copy to rush it in before the Angelus, I said:

'And the latest sports news is' — (pause) — 'Sorry — not — quite — sport — Hugh Gaitskill, the leader of the British Labour Party, has just died.' And up came the Angelus, leaving a bewildered public not knowing whether to laugh, say the Angelus or pray for the soul of the departed Mr Gaitskill. An over-enthusiastic sub-editor had taken the 'sports flash' route and had delivered his hot story under the door of the sports studio. You reach a point where, if you were to worry about embarrassment, you couldn't do the job, so you just rely on your sense of humour to get you through and the sense of humour of others to accept you.

I had one particularly ridiculous misuse of words in a table tennis commentary which my colleagues never let me forget. It was, I think, one of the first outdoor broadcasts of the minority sport of table tennis from the National Stadium in Dublin. It was a live morning telecast of an early round match between two elderly ladies from the North of Ireland who kept a steady ping-pong going in machine-like fashion for interminable periods, which was not calculated to rescue me from the arms of Morpheus into which I kept falling.

The previous day I had driven to Donegal to sing a couple of songs and assist in picking a local beauty queen. On the way home, somewhere in a remote area between Sligo and Boyle, I ran out of petrol. The story of how I was rescued in the late hours of the morning by a farmer who happened along and after sharing a bottle of Baby Power with me to ward off the cold, tied the bottle to a string and proceeded to take petrol from the tank of his own car and pour it into mine is, as they say, sceal eile. But I reached Dublin too late to get sleep before going live on air. I was the link man and the informed running commentator was the one and only Harry Thuillier who had represented Ireland at both table tennis and fencing in the Olympic Games. If there had been an Olympics for charm and fast talking, Harry would have been selected for those two.

A few days previously Harry had given me a book on table

tennis, so that I would have some idea of what he was talking about, and he particularly mentioned a section on the grip used by the Chinese. I read how they favoured the 'penhold' grip because it came naturally to them on account of the way they held their chopsticks when they were eating their rice. This had stayed with me, but between the mesmeric effect of the elderly ladies monotonously ping-ponging and my early morning escapades, I was on the verge of nodding off when I heard Harry say, 'Isn't that right Brendan?' Not getting an immediate reply, he looked around at me, saw my confusion and added: 'The Chinese favour the penhold grip.' 'Oh yes, Harry,' I said, and began to struggle towards remembering what I had read about the Chinese eating rice with their chopsticks. My difficulty was recalling the precise words. 'Oh yes, Harry. The Chinese hold the bat in the same way as they hold (and I couldn't think of chopsticks) their implements when they are eating their (what's this they eat?) spaghetti.'

Harry, for once in his life, was speechless. What could he say? After a suitable pause, he went ahead with the commentary and I don't think he called me in for further contributions. My embarrassment was eased when there were no calls to say the Chinese didn't eat spaghetti with their implements, which could mean either that nobody was watching, or those watching had also fallen asleep, or table tennis followers have a good sense of humour.

# Tony O'Reilly

In 1970 I travelled to Twickenham to play my final game for the Irish rugby team, a game for which I had written the programme notes. It had been sixteen years since my first cap, and eight years since my last, and not being exactly at the peak of my fitness, I was somewhat bewildered to find myself chosen.

At the final training session the day before the big game,

there was comment from some pundits as I was seen off the training ground by my chauffeur, Arthur Whelan. As Arthur opened the door to my car, the team left in their bus.

The sports writers and enthusiasts were as shocked as I was at my selection. The newspapers celebrated this latest demonstration of Irish lunacy, amazed at the decision to pick this 'elderly statesman'. A headline in a British newspaper said it all, 'Heinz Meanz Haz Beanz'. My chauffeur Arthur was also the subject of much comment. His picture appeared in nearly every paper.

Twickenham in the seventies was not a place for the faint hearted. The English team went on to win three triple-crowns that decade. For reasons best known to the selectors, I was the one chosen to replace the injured Irish wing, Willie Brown.

I was conscious of the fact that I had been in better shape, and this was not lost on other members of the team. The team captain, Willie John McBride, said to me on the morning of the game that my best attacking move today might be to 'shake my jowls at my opposite number to best terrify him'. So it wasn't a very encouraging start in the dressing room!

The match was largely uneventful, and one which we could have won but for a couple of long-range drop goals from their talented half-backs. At the very end of it I resorted to doing something I had avoided doing during my entire rugby career — I threw myself on the loose ball at the feet of a rather disagreeable group of English forwards. As the English pack passed over me, I received what centuries of Irish men had received from passing English men, a stiff tap on the back of the head. I was knocked unconscious.

As I was picked up by two ambulance men, I came to in this cacophony of sound. Although I could hear a great number of voices in the 80,000-strong crowd, I heard one voice in particular, a man with a broad Dublin accent, shouting 'And kick his bloody chauffeur while yer at it.'

# COLM O'ROURKE

Few people, I am sure, would be willing to reveal in print something which might have been truly embarrassing to them in case it would be used to poke fun at them at some later stage.

I have been fortunate in avoiding such situations as a rule, but have witnessed a few cases which some people would prefer not to have been part of. Perhaps the worst was the well-documented case of Terry Ferguson who pulled a muscle in his back togging out before the fourth Dublin-Meath game in 1991. The pain was so severe, Terry was crying out in agony, and it was only relieved by an injection in the back. So while we left the dressing room for the game, he was left lying on the bench to recover. While that was embarrassing enough for him, it must have been doubly so for his wife Lorraine, when she realised that her husband was not on the team. When she went to make enquiries as to the nature of the injury, she was informed that her Terry had injured himself taking off his trousers. Both Terry and Lorraine were the butt of many jokes for quite a while afterwards.

In my own case, there were a couple of incidents which other people found amusing, but which I had hoped could pass unnoticed. One was in a Leinster Championship against Kildare in Tullamore when I was injured but had togged out as a sub. Quite unwittingly, I joined the team photograph which made it then a total of sixteen players. As Meath won the All-Ireland that year the photo was reproduced on many occasions and some of the players eventually spotted the extra man. I got a lot of slagging for a while on being so vain that I still had to get into the team picture even when I was not part of the group.

A worse case than that happened in a club minor match when I was playing centre-field. As we attacked, I made a great diagonal run crossfield and somebody spotted the move and placed a great ball behind. But I ignored the ball and, still moving at great pace, left the pitch and headed at breakneck speed for the dressing room. I made the loo just in time and returned within a few minutes to take my place, much to the amusement of the opposition as well as my team mates. Fortunately, we won the match, so my fastest dash of the day was not too costly.

# SEAN O'ROURKE

Do they remember the question that I asked Mrs Thatcher at Hillsborough? How about the interview with F. W. de Klerk going backwards up the escalator? Or the day Martin McGuinness said the studio wasn't Castlereagh Interrogation Centre? As John Wayne might put it, the hell they do!

Oh no. But try asking about the day Joe O'Toole came on 'Morning Ireland'. They remember that one all right, as I've found to my discomfort many, many times. Everywhere from the fairground in Tramore to dinner parties in Dublin 4, it has given total strangers a conversation line, one that I'll never live down.

On 1 July 1993, the first day of the primary school year, the INTO criticised the Minister for Education for deciding that sixteen out of 200 teachers designated for primary schools in deprived areas should instead be used for pre-school education.

It should have been a straight pro-forma interview lasting three minutes or so. The General Secretary of the INTO would criticise Niamh Bhreathnach for diverting resources from the most underfunded primary sector in Europe; I would contend that children in deprived areas needed even earlier education. Not exactly the stuff of Jacob's Awards.

As usual, David Hanly and I were in at six o'clock. After

half an hour quietly studying the morning newspapers and the briefing material for 'Morning Ireland', we began the 'divvy-up' of items in the running order.

For no particular reason it was settled that I would interview O'Toole, with David wondering aloud about what quotable quote he would produce on the air later on. We both knew that Joe O'Toole would arrive well prepared, for he is not a man who leaves things to chance.

The item was scheduled after 'AA Roadwatch' and the sports news. Four of us were sitting at a small round desk in the cramped and dingy old Radio News studio. Now happily defunct, it was there that Garret FitzGerald had launched his famous Constitutional Crusade. From there, Charlie Haughey had launched more than one successful fightback against his foes.

Senator O'Toole was to my left, with Hanly on the right and Tony O'Donoghue directly opposite, politely remaining seated until the next ad-break after the sports slot was over. Little did he know!

Joe O'Toole accepted that pre-school education was a good thing in deprived areas, but it shouldn't be provided at the expense of the primary sector. He might have been expected to suggest the minister was 'robbing Peter to set up a system to pay Paul'.

But he didn't say that. No — that would be too predictable. After recalling that Ireland had the largest primary school classes in Europe, he combined sorrow with anger and said with gusto: 'We're chuggin' along with four bald tyres and the minister goes and sells the spare wheel in order to buy petrol.'

The quote! This was it! Momentarily, and fatally, I glanced sideways. Had David recognised it? The glint said he had, the twitch found a mirror around my mouth, and chaos ensued.

I tried and utterly failed to smother a chuckle that became a snigger before turning into a belly laugh. The harder I tried, the worse the urge became. As I lost control, poor

Tony O'Donoghue's eyes were agog with disbelief on the other side of the table.

Bravely, Senator O'Toole, his voice now catching also, tried to keep the show on the road, as it were. 'OK, we'll go along for a while, but we will eventually come to a halt . . .' He gulped some air. '. . . We'll grind to a halt.' The interviewer already had.

Panic stricken, I tried to say something coherent, only to hear myself utter the famous last words: 'Sorry, I think . . . ahem . . . you're . . . it's the way you tell 'em!'

Heroically, Joe O'Toole made another effort to rescue me. 'The problem as I see it . . .' He was hoping I'd straighten my face again. What a forlorn hope! Eventually the General Secretary of the INTO became the man who ran out of petrol himself as he too descended into embarrassed laughter and silence. It felt like for ever but lasted only seven seconds.

Clearly there was no way back from such disorder. David intervened to tell the listeners that people were collapsing all around him in the studio (an eloquent statement of the obvious) and that it was time to hear a tape about the strawberry fair in Enniscorthy.

Afterwards, I was to be convinced of two things: the exchange had added greatly to the gaiety of the nation that summer morning; and secondly, they were listening to 'Morning Ireland' in massive numbers. Those who weren't have since had the tape replayed on numerous occasions for their enjoyment.

Never before or since has the 'Playback' programme sought out an item with such alacrity. In so far as tapes can breed, this one was a big buck rabbit. I have never willingly listened to it again since that day. Sure, I saw the funny side (isn't that why it happened in the first place) but the incident did neither of us any good. And it wouldn't want to happen again.

# MAUREEN POTTER

It was 1960 and I went to the Gaiety to see the great Orson Welles in *Chimes at Midnight*, excerpts from Shakespeare's 'Henry' plays. After the show, I nipped backstage to congratulate a few old friends who were in it. When I reached the Green Room, I found the full cast still in costume standing there, apparently waiting for some VIP visit. I did not want to intrude and I was slipping quietly out of the room when I was confronted by the ample figure of Hilton Edwards. He pushed me back into the Green Room and introduced me in the most effusive, flattering terms to his companion, Laurence Olivier. Laurence Olivier was one of my idols, but I expected nothing more than a quick handshake, as he was obviously coming to meet Orson Welles and the cast.

But Hilton had other ideas. He bubbled on at great length about my many years in the Gaiety, my association with Jimmy O'Dea, how much Michael admired me, and so on and so on. Laurence Olivier nodded politely, but I could see from the glazed look in his eyes that he was wondering what this woman had to do with the show and why he had to meet her. I could see the cast, mostly English, fidgeting around, puzzled as to what was going on. Worse still, I could see Orson Welles, still in his Falstaff costume, positively pawing the ground like an anxious stallion. As for me, I was hoping the floor would open up and swallow me. If only I was on stage I could nod to the stage manager, he would press the button and I would disappear through the Gaiety trapdoor. But still Hilton rattled on.

Orson Welles could stand it no longer. He strode across the room, embraced Larry, and practically manhandled him over to meet the cast. He glared at me as he passed, the full Citizen Kane glare, but I can assure you I was far more embarrassed than he was annoyed. Hilton Edwards was the kindest, most courteous of men, a dear friend, a gifted director, but that night in my beloved Gaiety he produced my most embarrassing experience.

# PADDY POWER

*The Day I Didn't See Red*

Even though I am some years retired from politics at national level, I am still a member of Kildare County Council and keep my hand in locally in a leisurely fashion. We have, in my parish, a motor-racing circuit in Mondello Park, and while an attempt to hold Feile there in 1995 was strongly and successfully resisted, I would not like to see the track closing, as it is the only one in Ireland.

So, when I got a phone call from a nice young lady with a request to meet her to discuss the future of Mondello, I accepted her invitation to join her for lunch in the Naas Court Hotel.

Dressed in my best dark blue suit and white shirt, I sallied forth for my date with Orla. She was a very enthusiastic and vivacious young lady with quite a few proposals for the future of the track. Some of these were matters for solving at County Council level and I promised to help.

Another suggestion was that any motorist whose driving licence was revoked should undergo a driving test before being allowed on to the public road again. This was obviously controversial, but Orla hoped that such unfortunates would avail of the facilities in Mondello to have their driving skills renewed before attempting the test. This was a matter of policy at a higher level and little did I think that a minister would contemplate such a move and cause much anxiety later to a motorist who might fail the breathalyser test and have to undergo a driving test — probably the first in a lifetime of driving.

After a lovely lunch and a few drinks, Orla and I parted on

good terms and I sauntered down the main street to my parked car. It was a sunny afternoon and many locals greeted me with a happy smile or a cheery nod. I thought to myself, Naas is a nice town and you only have to walk down the street to realise it.

Just then a coloured man approached and said with a toothy grin: 'You appear to be a very happy man and a distinguished man too, if I may say so.'

'I am a happy man,' I replied, 'because I'm taking life easy now that I'm retired.'

'What! Retired at 45?' he exclaimed in mock disbelief.

Being a suspicious person and feeling that this piece of flattery was the prelude to a request for a fiver, I thought it best to keep moving towards my car with a parting remark, 'Thanks for your courtesy and good luck to you too!'

My good humour continued as I drove home, humming a few bars of a song, and I found my own family just finishing their lunch in the kitchen.

I announced: 'I met a very perceptive man in Naas who said I appeared to be a happy man and a distinguished man too.'

This was greeted by unruly laughter and Patsy brought me down to earth with, 'No wonder he said that. Have a look at yourself.'

On looking down I saw the bright red serviette from the Naas Court Hotel still stuck in my waist-band and hanging in a very obvious and eye-catching triangle on my trousers pocket.

My face matched the colour of the forgotten napkin and I revised my opinion of the nice Naas natives.

# MAURICE PRATT

When I was growing up my mother had frequent reason to say to us, 'Sticks and stones may break my bones, but names will never hurt me', which is probably not surprising when you have a surname like Pratt, which rhymes with words like 'brat' etc.

One of the embarrassing moments which stands out in my mind had to do with a misunderstanding of my name. It happened when I arrived at the home of my wife-to-be (Pauline) on our very first date. As I was to find out subsequently, Pauline had more than one boyfriend at the time, and the Christian name of one of those boyfriends was Pat. When I arrived at her house, I was shown into the living-room where her grandmother was watching television along with Pauline's younger sisters. At least twice during the following ten minutes her grandmother said to me, 'You're Pat now, aren't you?' and I replied, 'Pratt. That's right, Pratt.' Fortunately, she was hard of hearing and didn't pick up what I was saying. If she had, perhaps I'd have taken a fit of pique and would not be very happily married today with five children.

By the way, during my conversation with Pauline's grandmother the living-room door was open and Pauline and her older sister, Betty, were in convulsions of laughter in the kitchen.

I wasn't embarrassed about any of this at the time but, subsequently, whenever reminded about it, my cheeks always turn pink.

There is a second incident which also stands out in my mind. It happened in 1979 when I was in my early twenties. I was involved in the organising of a black tie dinner in Jury's Hotel, and when the function was under way and the meal was being served, I repaired to the Coffee Dock along with a few colleagues for a well-earned break. We were all dressed in tuxedos and had been sitting down for about fifteen minutes when we were approached at the table by a young boy of about 7 who said to me, 'Can I have your autograph, please?' (Now, bear in mind this happened at least five years before I appeared on television.) I mumbled something to the child, not having a clue who he thought I was. Somebody at the next table who was observing the incident shouted over, 'Ah, go on Johnny, don't be such a louse. Sign the autograph for the kid.'

Then the penny dropped. The young lad thought I was Johnny Logan and so I sent the child away happy with an autograph for himself and his two sisters. (Did I really look like Johnny Logan!)

# TERRY PRONE

*The Worm that (Nearly) Ate my Trike*

We're not talking ordinary trike, here. Ordinary toddlers' trikes had little itty-bitty pedals stuck on the front wheel and they just turned that front wheel and looked like they fell out of a Noddy book.

This trike had serious pedals and a *chain* and wheels with spokes. It was red. I was 4.

The pride. The speed. The new status in the area — heck, if someone had arrived home with a Porsche, they'd have been muck compared to me and my trike.

All morning, on the day it arrived, I rode it up and down the path outside the front doors of the houses on our road, to let the neighbours express the wonder and admiration I knew they felt. Also to educate them. It's just amazing the essential features a 40-year old will miss when praising a trike. I did demonstrations of the horn and showed them how the metal protector of the chain meant I could not get oil on my white socks. (They forbore to point out that this only applied to my right ankle. The chain not being protected on the other side, my left ankle-sock was already black by lunchtime, but left ankles are just not as important, in the scheme of things, as right ankles.)

When lunchtime came, panic set in. There could be no doubt that the word had gone out that Terry Prone had a new trike which was the envy of the world, and robbers would be already lurking in every porch, hiding behind the empty milk bottles, just waiting their chance to snatch it and make for the hills. With it, if not on it.

'Calm down,' my mother said. 'We'll take it round the back.'

The world for me at that time was divided into Out the Front and Round the Back, the connection between them being a little side passage between our house and Dowdall's. I took the trike down the side passage and parked it where, helped by a cushion underneath me to raise me higher in the chair, I could keep an eye on it during lunch.

The minute lunch was over, I was out again, going around and around the back garden on it, doing three-point turns like an L-plate driver practising for a driving test. Occasionally I'd leave it for a few minutes and go for a quick spin on our swing, but even then I'd leave its front wheel canted around as if it was looking at me.

It was after one of those go's on the swing that the threat appeared. It was huge. One of the biggest I had ever seen. Shiny, moist and with circular scar tissue on it suggesting it had a fighting — and winning — past. It was a worm.

I went roaring into the kitchen.

'Going to eat my tricycle', I bellowed through my tears, pointing frantically out the back door.

Mother, father and big sister all plunged out the back door to find out *what* was going to ingest my new vehicle.

'There's nothing there', my sister said, and went back to her apple tart.

'Is SO!' I howled, a trembling finger indicating the monster.

'It's a worm', my father said, baffled.

'NOW!' I said, since his comment proved my point.

'Worms don't eat trikes', he said and went back to his coffee.

I stood there, racked by sobs, watching the worm undulating ever more meaningfully towards my beloved trike. My mother went down on her hunkers beside me.

'D'you remember Sara the elephant in the zoo?'

I nodded, speechless with grief.

'Well, could you eat Sara?'

I shook my head, tears splashing to right and left.

'Sara would be too big for you to eat, right? Well, your trike is just too big for the worm to eat.'

At this moment, the worm lifted its head, examined the trike (I figured he was working out could he at least eat a wheel or two) and undulated back where he came from. I clutched my mother in gratitude. It was all over.

Or so I thought. How was I going to know that every year for forty years afterwards, whenever there was a family argument, *someone* would, at some point, announce, 'We all know Terry has no sense of proportion. D'you remember the worm going to eat her tricycle?'

It silences me. Every time, it silences me.

Especially because, to this day, I secretly believe he would have. The only reason he didn't was he was afraid of my mother . . .

# FEARGAL QUINN

'Kenny Live' is a must for a great number of television viewers every Saturday night. It has been a success for both Pat Kenny and RTE for some years now. But it was not born as 'Kenny Live' — at its birth it was 'Saturday Live' with a different presenter each week. The idea was that the presenter would not be a TV professional and would put his or her own chat programme together.

Paul Cusack was the producer who explained the concept to me back in September 1986. I love a challenge and readily accepted the invitation to be the presenter of the first programme. In the following few weeks, I started selecting my guests, telephoning them to coax them to come on to 'my' programme.

It was a few weeks before the programme that Paul Cusack added the idea that the presenters were expected to do a 'party piece' of their own.

'You know,' Paul explained, 'everyone can sing a song, do a recitation, or just make funny faces.'

Now my problem is that anyone who has heard me sing has very little regard for my ability to keep in tune. I told Paul this, but he persisted. 'You must be good at something.'

'Well, I can cook mussels,' I answered. 'In fact, I think my mussels are beyond reproach.'

'OK,' he said, 'that's it. We'll provide the cooker and you can cook mussels live on TV.'

So the big day arrived.

I thought the programme was going quite well — that just shows how pride always comes before a big tumble. I introduced my next guest, Phil Coulter, but said, 'Before Phil plays for you let me do my party piece', and proceeded to demonstrate my culinary expertise on the brand new cooker that RTE had provided with words like 'It's so easy — even a man could do it', and 'Nothing can go wrong, and now Phil Coulter will play for you for the next four minutes whilst my mussels will simmer away. Ladies and gentlemen, Phil Coulter.'

As the cameras focused on Phil playing the piano, I got the distinct smell — not of mussels but of burning rubber. I had not tested the new cooker and it had blown the fuse after burning the flex. The beautiful food I had prepared lay flat and cold and very unappetising in the saucepan.

My words 'Nothing can go wrong' bounced back at me.

Shall I call it a day and admit that things can go wrong even with a simple recipe?

Well, I decided to bluff it out, pretended that the dish was a success, offered samples to my guests who included my cousin Ruairi Quinn, TD, and Baroness Detta O'Cathain. They showed no enthusiasm for cold uncooked mussels whilst I braved it out by eating the unappetising food with comments like 'Aren't those oysters just delicious!'

It wasn't until my wife, Denise, interrupted from the front row to tell me that they were mussels and not oysters that I decided to change the subject and introduce my next guest.

As a matter of record, here is the recipe:

### Mussels — the French way

Buy at least 1 lb per person (a friend of mine would eat more than 100!) and soak them in the sink. Discard any open or floating mussels. Resoak them in cold water, removing the moustache. Prepare six cloves of garlic (trust me) in a little Flora, with the same number of shallots, by gently simmering.

Add half a bottle of cheap white wine and a tablespoon of mustard.
When these have simmered gently, add the mussels.
Add 6 bay leaves.
Boil furiously for one minute.
Remove from heat and let all the flavours mingle. Serve.

# MICK QUINN

*Ireland 9 Wales 9   Lansdowne Road, 1974.*

1974 was a very successful season for Ireland in that we won the International Championship, being the only team to win away from home that season when we beat England in a classic game at Twickenham 26–21 (4 tries to 1). We lost to France narrowly at Parc des Princes 9–6, and beat a lively Scotland 9–6.

The Welsh were very strong, with J. P. R. Williams, Gerard Davies, J. J. Williams, Phil Bennett and Gareth Edwards in their backline. Mervyn Davies was their star forward, and he was ably supported by Bobby Windsor, Graham Price, Dai Morris and Terry Colsner.

We were a good side, brilliantly led by Willie John McBride, and in an inexperienced pack we had Ken Kennedy, Ray McLoughlin, Moss Keane, Fergus Slattery and Shay Deering. The star back was Mike Gibson, the best player I ever played with. My scrum-half was Johnny Moloney, an excellent player, and we always teamed up well.

Johnny and I sort of looked alike, and even now people mistake me for him and vice versa. 'How ya Johnny!' is a regular greeting to me.

Immediately following the match against Wales, one we were very unlucky not to win as we had dominated for most of the game, we were in the tea rooms of the old Lansdowne pavilion before departing for our hotel. A young boy came up to me brandishing an autograph book and pen. 'Gee, Johnny, can I have your autograph please?' I hadn't the heart to say, 'Look I'm not Johnny Moloney. I'm Mick Quinn.' So I signed 'To Brian, best wishes, Johnny Moloney.' The boy turned to me and said, 'Thanks a million, Johnny, but tell me something. How do you play with yer man Mick Quinn? He's crap!'

# ALBERT REYNOLDS

*Comedy of Errors*

In 1981, as Minister for Transport, I was invited to launch the new CIE Bombardier bus in Shannon. Kathleen and I were on our way back from Cork, where she had just launched the new B & I Ferry, *Leinster*, without a hitch. Throughout the journey she joked that the pressure was on me to perform just as well as she had done.

The ceremony in Shannon began with the usual cracking of the bottle of champagne. Once the guests were safely out of range, I began, 'I am pleased . . .' and gave the bottle a forceful swing for good measure.

At that time, however, the Lord Mayor, who was slightly late, was trying to discreetly place himself among the crowd by coming in from behind the bus. His plan came to an abrupt halt as the bottle hit the bus but exploded in the Lord Mayor's face. The champagne destroyed his suit and the glass left him with minor cuts on his face.

After the Mayor had received medical attention and my deepest apologies, the guests embarked on the bus. My next task was to drive the bus out of the factory — quite simple, but not on this occasion. The bus wouldn't start. After many attempts the mechanics were called in and eventually I succeeded in driving the bus out of the factory.

At this point a professional driver took over from me and our destination was the Limerick Inn Hotel. However, halfway there the bus broke down. Everybody had to abandon ship (bus). The media, who were following behind, couldn't believe their luck. What a sight! The Minister for Transport, the Chairman of CIE and all the other guests having to bail out of the new CIE Bombardier bus on the side of the road and find alternative means of transport to the hotel. After many snapshots we eventually made it to the Limerick Inn.

That evening everybody settled down to watch the News, and waited in anticipation to see the débâcle appear on the screen. Nothing appeared. No one could figure it out — hints of censorship maybe? However, the next morning the newspapers had a field day — four pictures on the front page of one of the national newspapers.

Later that week I met one of the RTE correspondents who covered the launch. He admitted that the tape had failed to function that evening. Were the gremlins at work?

'What a disaster! What a comedy of errors!' he laughed.

To which I replied, 'Comedy of Errors has always been good to me. He won the Champion Hurdle at Cheltenham three years in a row.'

# DESMOND RUSHE

Nobody, I imagine, would write honestly about the most embarrassing moment experienced. For one thing, it could be too embarrassing to write about: not all embarrassments have a lighter side, either at the time or in retrospect. The embarrassments of which I write are not too embarrassing to write about: one of them was observed, and one was experienced. Both were embarrassing at the time, though not painfully so.

The setting for the first, which was observed, is Dublin Castle, where a reception is in progress. Michael Mac Liammoir, now almost totally blind, is there and, feeling tired, he goes to sit on a chair beside the wall. Unfortunately someone has left a tray of canapés on the chair, and when Michael sits, he squelches together cubes of cheese, green grapes which have been cut in half, biscuits and cod's roe masquerading as caviare. A mild sensation is created in the vicinity of the incident when Michael feels the moisture of squashed delicacies seep through the seat of his pants.

'Before I sat down', he later says, 'the chair struck me as having remarkably colourful upholstery: it looked quite out of place in the state apartments.'

Michael Mac Liammoir also features in the experienced embarrassment. We had both been invited to a function in Castletown House which featured a theatrical presentation and a buffet meal. After the theatricals, we made our way to the nether regions of the house, where the buffet was being served, and I saw a table set for two, with a bottle of wine and plates laden with such things as cold turkey and ham, potato salad and beetroot. The Friends of Castletown House had been on the job, I thought, and we sat down to the free meal invited guests are entitled to expect.

We had filled our glasses and tucked into the food when I felt a presence close at hand. A military-type man with a pointed moustache was regarding us coldly, as was the elderly lady at his side. 'We don't mind you eating our food and drinking our wine', he said with heavy irony. From the look on his face and the tone of his voice what he really said was: you are a pair of thieves and you have stolen our supper. He had, it appeared, chosen and paid for the victuals and selected a suitable table before going to find his wife, who was now shooting invisible icicles at me with her eyes.

When I had swallowed the dollop of food I had in my mouth, I redressed my psychologically disadvantaged position and stood up. Explanations and apologies followed, but I felt the military-type gentleman found them singularly unconvincing. I offered to fill new plates and get another bottle of wine, but the offer was refused. I was left with no alternative but to offer payment for the purloined goods and was terrified I mightn't have enough money (Mac Liammoir had long since fallen into the agreeable practice of never carrying money, other than very small change). But I had enough, and after I had settled the account the military-type gentleman and his partner marched out without giving the buffet counter a glance. Obviously they had lost their appetites: some people have no sense of humour, or of the absurd.

# TIM RYAN

*Meeting a Familiar Face*

It is easy to tell when I am embarrassed. Many people can hide it very well. But me, no. I simply turn scarlet. I am a complete give-away. It happens, for example, when I meet somebody I know in a place where I'd rather not meet them. So, as my old *Evening Press* colleague and hero, Con Houlihan, would write, 'Now read on.'

When I finished secondary school in the early 1970s I studied for an arts degree in University College, Cork, and returned home to my native town a brand new teacher. I got a job in the local Mercy convent as a teacher of English, where I was just one of two males on the staff. I was quite friendly with the principal, Sr Emmanuel (not her real name) and, to be honest, the other male teacher, Des, and I were resented by the female staff who thought we always got special treatment from the principal on such issues as rostering and so on.

This was totally untrue, of course!

Sr Emmanuel liked me, not least because she had taught my older sister as a pupil some years before.

After a few years I decided I wanted to try some other career and got a job with a voluntary organisation. I said goodbye to Sr Emmanuel, Des, the female staff, the pupils, and left the school. Much to my surprise, shortly afterwards I heard that Sr Emmanuel herself had left the convent — and her job — and had gone to live in the outside world after thirty-five years as a nun. (I must point out the timing of both our departures was purely coincidental!) It must have been a very tough decision for her to make as a middle-aged woman, and I greatly admired her for it. It was a small rural town and, given the attitude of the nuns and public, sadly, there was no way she could have kept her job. Suddenly, Sr Emmanuel found herself out in the real world and unemployed, having been a school principal just a few short hours before.

Meanwhile, all was not going too well for me in my new job and I left it within nine months. I looked around for a while wondering what I might do. I considered going back to teaching, but in a school away from my home town. I applied for a job with North Tipperary VEC which had a vacancy for a teacher of English in Nenagh, and was duly called to interview.

And so one sunny morning I arrived in Nenagh and sat alone in a room waiting for what seemed like hours for the interview. Then suddenly, pity my situation, who should enter the room, also waiting for interview, but the former Sr Emmanuel, now dressed in a smart suit!

I turned scarlet with embarrassment! I have no recollection of the conversation. My contribution must have been very incoherent as I was not thinking straight. I was doubly embarrassed. Firstly for myself, I wondered how I would explain what had happened the new 'high-flying' job I had gone to, and why I was sitting waiting for an interview to be an English teacher, of all things! Secondly, I felt embarrassment for Sr Emmanuel as I had not spoken to her since she left the convent.

In any event, my incoherence must have continued at the interview because I did not get the job! I don't know if the former Sr Emmanuel ever got it either. I never checked. That morning I prayed that she would get it as she was far more entitled to it, and more experienced than I was. I understand she later taught in a school in the south-east where she married. I presume she is now retired. As for myself, I never went teaching again, and soon afterwards went into journalism where I finally found my niche.

I will always remember that August morning in 1980 in the small room in Nenagh Vocational School. I think of it every time I drive through Nenagh and smile to myself when I wonder who *did* get the teaching job?

# PATRICIA SCANLAN

My most embarrassing moment that is printable happened to me a few years ago when I was in hospital in the Bon Secours in Glasnevin. I was chatting to another patient and she pointed to the apartments in River Gardens.

'I'd love one of those,' she said.

'I used to live there. I just sold mine last week,' I told her.

She asked me all about them and I told her how I'd bought mine during a property slump when apartments had been selling very cheaply. I'd sold it at a good profit.

A few days later, after my operation, the man I sold the apartment to came to visit me. He brought me a beautiful big bouquet of flowers. We were chatting away and the woman I'd been speaking to was getting ready to leave hospital. She came over to me, threw her arms around me and said, 'Patricia, I wish you all the luck in the world and I hope you make as big a profit the next time you sell, as you did with your apartment.'

What could I say? My cheeks were as red as the roses in the bouquet, but he was a real gentleman and he made no comment at all. Still I was mortified and I was very relieved when a nurse came to give me an injection and he had to leave. I wasn't the better of it for ages!

# DES SMITH

It was the 1976 British Open and I had successfully pre-qualified as a young pro. This was a very big moment for me. I arrived on the first tee six or seven minutes before my tee-off, collected my card, wished my partners good luck etc. and settled myself before the all important first drive. While I was warming up, I noticed that the big stand next to the first tee was full, which made me a little more nervous than I already was. What I did not know was that the game following us included my great hero, Jack Nicklaus.

Jack arrived on the tee before we hit off. When it came to my turn, I was so nervous I had difficulty getting the ball on the tee. I then attempted to compose myself and play my all important first drive in the 1976 Open. Next thing I remember, I was walking off the teeing ground. I had to ask my caddie where I had hit the ball.

To this day, between nerves, the occasion, and Jack Nicklaus, I cannot remember seeing the club or hitting the shot. So when people talk about being nervous, I know exactly what they mean and what effect it sometimes has.

# RAYMOND SMITH

*'The Bonfires will Blaze in Moynalty.'*

I had one of my most embarrassing and at the same time funniest experiences as a journalist in the aftermath of Monksfield's triumph in the Champion Hurdle of 1978.

I had won enough money in ante-post bets and on the course itself to cause the celebratory mood to last well and beyond the victory dinner thrown by Monksfield's owner, Galway-born Dr Michael Mangan in the Queen's Hotel, where I was staying.

Monksfield was going home and, as I adjourned to my room, I knew that all the Alka Seltzer in the world would not save me from waking with some 'head' in the morning. I made the time though to jot down the intro for my *Evening Herald* story . . . 'The bonfires will blaze in Moynalty this evening as Monksfield comes home to a hero's welcome.' I then put in a time call for 8.30 a.m.

I awoke with a splitting headache. I called the *Herald*, got the copy-taker and was beginning to ad lib the rest of my story after the colourful intro, when the news editor interjected to say: 'Cut the crap, Smith . . . forget about the bonfires and all that . . . Do you realise the racing is off because of the snow?'

My God, snow! What the hell is happening? Such were the thoughts running through my head in a mad whirl. Everything I had conjured up about bands and cheering crowds and bonfires lighting the hills around Moynalty went out the window in a flash.

Or rather, I came back to earth with a bang when I drew back the curtains and looked outside and saw the carpet of white. I was being told from Dublin what I would have known if I had been up at cock-crow.

There was a new urgency in the news editor's voice when he conveyed to me that the *Evening Herald* was being inundated with calls from punters who had coupled Champion Hurdle winner, Monksfield, with Brown Lad to win the Gold Cup, and they wanted to know what was going to happen their ante-post wagers. 'Give us a story fast', he said.

I must have broken the Irish hop, step and jump record as I skipped it down the stairs and, as luck would have it, collared Ladbroke's man in the foyer. I was able to put over a new story, quoting authoritative sources in the bookmaking world, that would satisfy every punter from Ballyfermot to Ballybofey and beyond that their money wasn't automatically lost, but that, assuming the Gold Cup was opened again, the doubles would become singles as it would, in effect, be a new race.

I was back in the good books of the News desk who, I must admit, were rather surprised how quickly I managed to get in contact with those authoritative sources. But I was rather sad that my lovely intro about the bonfires blazing around Moynalty in County Meath, where Monksfield was trained by Des McDonagh, got lost in that carpet of white snow.

For the record, the Irish punters who had been singing 'Brown Lad in the rain . . .' in anticipation of a famous triumph for the Jim Dreaper-trained gelding (winner of the Sun Alliance Novices Hurdle in 1974 and the Bonusprint Stayers Hurdle in 1975) were cruelly denied a clean-out of the bookies when the Cheltenham stewards, instead of putting racing back on the scheduled third day for twenty-four hours, refixed the Gold Cup for 12 April. On good ground that did not favour him, Brown Lad finished runner-up to Midnight Court, the mount of John Francome.

Raymond Smith writes now for the *Sunday Independent* and is author of the racing books, *Vincent O'Brien — The Master of Ballydoyle*, *The High Rollers of the Turf* and *Tigers of the Turf*, and also of his autobiography, *Urbi Et Orbi And All That*.

# SAM SMITH

Where I grew up, the older lads saw the GAA as mildly exotic yet potentially threatening: maybe a bit like a soccer hooligan's view of a Clare man with a cricket bat. And the first time I heard hurling and Gaelic football dismissed as 'stickball' and 'bogball' was from an apostle of the *Hot Press* generation, a native Athlonian who embraced Lou Reed and Manchester United as role models rather than Big Tom and Christy Ring.

Back in the mid-1970s, a couple of years after moving to Dublin from Belfast, I embraced the joyful mysteries of Gaelic football with the zeal of a convert. Cathal O'Shea, a Dublin-born son of proud Kerry parents, was my reluctant GAA godfather, responsible for educating me in the game that was a religion in the kingdom of football deities from which the O'Sheas emigrated a generation earlier. Instructing an ignorant Northern Prod on the subtleties and beauty of a great game must have been a wearisome task, but the stoic O'Shea persevered. My friend Cathal had no tug of loyalties through those epic tussles between Dublin and Kerry: his support for the kingdom never wavered through those four unforgettable seasons that ended the 1970s. Looking back, other friends must have squirmed with embarrassment for me and my unswerving loyalty to my adopted new home. Yet, my new-found enthusiasm for Gaelic football was confined to the spectacle: when it came to participating, I agreed with another Dub, Oscar Wilde, that 'Football is all very well as a game for rough girls, but it is hardly suitable for delicate boys.'

Working as *Sunday World* gum shoe reporters, Cathal and I had a ritual on those All-Ireland final and semi-final days from 1976 to 1979: we would beg tickets or bluff our way into Croke Park for the match, then argue *en route* to Pat Hourican's pub in Leeson Street, drink pints, discuss the game, get drunk, and then repeat the same conversation more or less verbatim until lights out.

A late education compounds the truism 'a little knowledge is a dangerous thing' and, as a Johnny-come-lately-GAA-know-all, I must have been a dangerous provocation to the most mild-mannered Gaelic football fan.

In 1976 Heffo's heroes stuffed Mick O'Dwyer's men 3–8 to 10 points in the final and it is still a tribute to Cathal O'Shea's long suffering good humour that he didn't respond with extreme violence to my ill-informed taunting after the game. And my post-match etiquette and swagger wasn't improved when the Dubs drubbed Kerry in the 1977 semi-final.

In 1978, even in the world beyond GAA, things began to get ugly: the Shah put Iran under martial law, and Pope John Paul I died after thirty-three days in office. These omens augured ill for a rookie Gaelic football fan whose attitude in Hourican's pub after the two previous Dublin-Kerry championship games could have been clinical case studies of the triumphalism of ignorance.

Cathal's brother Des and his pal, Mike Carty, got us stand tickets for the 1978 final. And in a masterclass in Gaelic footballing wizardry, an inspired Kerry team dominated the game, leaving a frustrated Dublin defence with bad-tempered obstruction as their only tactic. From the Hogan Stand, it seemed that blonde-haired and angel-faced Dr Pat O'Neill, at his robust best, was demolishing Kerry midfielders like a choirboy with a lump hammer. Dublin's granite-jawed and clean-limbed Corinthian princes roamed Croke Park experimenting in what future sporting anthropologists may judge as 'early athletic ethnic cleansing'. But the Serbian strategy didn't change a historic inevitability: Kerry won convincingly.

At the end of the game the O'Sheas simply smiled, but their silent, patronising, magnanimity in victory seemed just a cunning Kerry tactic designed to deepen my psychic shock. Back in Hourican's pub, I sat at the counter and defended Dublin's honour to the grinning O'Sheas who darkened my humour by illuminating to passers-by my ignorance of Gaelic football.

Around eight o'clock, when I was making more pathetic excuses for the Dublin team's on-field gratuitous violence to Cathal O'Shea, I turned 180 degrees to the man who had just sat down beside me at the bar counter. His short, fair hair was neat, he was freshly shaved and he wore a crisp white shirt and sober tie beneath a natty tweed jacket. I assumed he was one of those bright young thirtyish men who go into Hourican's on weekdays from the Department of Foreign Affairs, or from one of the corporate law firms around St Stephen's Green. Although he was in conversation with someone else, I rather rudely interrupted him and asked if he had seen the game? Yes, he replied. Would he not agree that while spirited, the Dublin team's defensive tactics were dictated by the unexpected change of tactics, speed and aggression of the Kerry team?

His shy smile was augmented with a puzzled look as he tried to make up his mind if I was metaphorically tweaking his nose or pulling his leg. I suppose my northern accent must have satisfied him I was just another lounge-bar-know-all-bore, and he resigned himself good naturedly to the inevitable. Yes, he said quietly, he had been at the game and Kerry had played well, but Dublin had played their hearts out too. He skilfully avoided the subject of physical tackling, and reckoning that he may be a useful ally to burst the beatifically happy O'Shea brothers' bubble, I pressed him harder. But with the practised panache of a street-wise politician, he orally ducked and verbally weaved, stubbornly refusing to be drawn on any suggestion of dirty play by the Dublin team.

I turned back to face the O'Sheas, but they had moved further down the bar. Anxious to recruit my new friend's views in support of my own post-match analysis, I called Cathal O'Shea over to join us — but he gestured for me to come to him.

'Do you know who you're talking to?' asked O'Shea, with an air of long suffering resignation.

'Yes,' I replied, 'that blonde-haired guy in the sports coat.'

'That,' said O'Shea, 'is Dr Pat O'Neill.'

The anaesthetic did nothing to dull that frozen blinding moment of revelation when we see ourselves as others see us: on that Sunday in September 1978, I was a gauche, gibbering, know-all fool.

I keep my own counsel in sports discussions now, although I have observed the three general elections since 1987 and frequently share my forthright views on current affairs with the readers of the *Irish Independent* — not much has changed.

# MICHAEL SMURFIT

L ike so many people of my vintage, I have no shortage of embarrassing stories from the past. I'm pretty sure I would want most of them to remain unknown. In any case, for charity, I am prepared to recall two stories.

The first brought me quite a lot of public embarrassment and a lot of enjoyment to my colleagues. It occurred just after the company had completed the acquisition of Time Industries, our first major US investment, in September 1974. After a gruelling few weeks of negotiations and meetings, we rewarded ourselves with a day off and a visit to Disneyland. That evening I hosted a dinner for management at a local entertainment spot within the complex. My first embarrassment was clear on my arrival at the restaurant, when my decision to wear a suit and tie conflicted with everyone else's to come casual. This would have been enough, had it not also transpired that I was to be set up by my own management during the evening.

After the meal was completed and the entertainment was about to start, my name was called out to go up to the podium. When I reached the stage, I was accosted by a number of 'Red Indians' and forced to dress up as a Red Indian for the Cowboy and Indian show — perhaps the first ever Chief Sitting Bull in a suit!

My father, Jefferson Smurfit, had an embarrassing incident with my brother Jeff, Jnr. My mother had insisted he work during his summer holidays and he agreed on the basis that his friend could also work with him. One particular day the shift manager on duty and my father went on a tour of inspection. My father was a hard worker and expected the same of those around him.

You can imagine his embarrassment when be came upon Jeff, hiding behind a pallet of board, playing cards with his pal. Although Jeff had cleared the cards by the time my father appeared, it was clear they were up to something. In order that he was not seen to show favouritism, he berated Jeff and asked him to explain what he was doing. Jeff replied that he was doing nothing.

He turned to the friend: 'And what the hell are you doing?' To which the friend replied, 'I'm helping him!'

# PAT SPILLANE

As a footballer, I suppose it should be very easy to recall many embarrassing moments: missing a sitter in the last minute of an All-Ireland final or letting the ball drop through your hands to concede a soft goal to the opposition and then being for ever remembered in folklore when one recalls those finals as the day Spillane blundered and cost us the match. Thankfully, during my career as a Gaelic footballer, such few embarrassing moments were not executed before the gaze of 70,000 people in Croke Park, but usually before a dozen people, a couple of dogs and the grazing sheep around my local club pitch in Templenoe, quickly forgotten about amongst the usual litany of blunders conceded by the club players and most definitely never recorded for posterity.

It is very difficult to recall one particular embarrassing moment that really stands out, but in my career as a teacher in St Goban's College, Bantry, Co. Cork, I can certainly think of many such occasions which would certainly be deserving of the title, 'my most embarrassing moment'. Whatever about embarrassing moments in public, where there is a chance to get away with it and it's quickly forgotten, youngsters in class will not hesitate to bring you back down to earth; and if you think an embarrassing moment or blunder will be forgotten about quickly, you can forget it. As long as you teach in a school, you will be continually reminded of them. How thoughtful they are!

Many embarrassing moments as a teacher spring to mind: awarding Cathy O'Sullivan 80 per cent for her geography test and then sending the report home, stating that she is an excellent student, particularly good on the physical geography aspect of the course, only to discover she has opted instead to do French for the Leaving and has not been in your geography class for at least two years.

Parent/teacher meetings, which are some of the worst days of teachers' lives (and certainly a justifiable reason for early retirement), provide more than their fair share of embarrassing moments. Mrs O'Sullivan is enquiring about her son John's progress: should he be doing pass or honours and is he well behaved in class. Quite a reasonable query, you might think, and probably if it was up around County Louth, with so few O'Sullivans in class, you could give an accurate and honest reply. Not so down in west Cork, where there are at least 70 O'Sullivans in the school and at least half a dozen of those are named, yes, you've guessed it, John. Having carefully answered all Mrs O'Sullivan's queries that he is doing excellently in class, a definite honours student and by far the best athlete in P. E. class, she then casually informs you that her John is the one in remedial class, who also, because of his ill health, is unable to compete in sport or any physical activity. Oh Jaysus, not that John O'Sullivan!

Probably the most embarrassing moment I faced as a teacher was when a colleague and I decided to organise the first ever foreign school tour to Paris. For reasons which you will shortly discover, and to protect his good name, my colleague shall remain anonymous. No stone was left unturned in organising the tour: the best of accommodation in Paris, a boat trip on the Seine, the best of cabins on the ferry. Their first school tour, their first ever trip outside Ireland, was eagerly anticipated by these bright-eyed youngsters.

At last the great day arrived, early morning excitement, the children all in new clothes, name tags in place, mothers hugging and caressing them, putting the final touches to their appearance, some suitcases so big they could have taken all Scott's equipment to the Antarctic with room to spare.

The clock ticked expectantly to nine o'clock, the eagerly awaited departure time, the rest of the school all assembled to wave us off on our momentous journey. 9.30 came and went, the bus late, still no worries. 10.30, slight nervousness and apprehension. Where was the bus? Nothing to worry about, kids consoled by telling them we had allowed for plenty of time to get to Rosslare and have a couple of pit stops on the way. 11.30 and panic bells began to ring. Did the bus break down? Had the tour company forgotten to arrange a bus?

Ring the tour company frantically, going to give them a piece of our mind . . . This was no way to treat good customers . . . Call this a service . . . You will be hearing from our solicitors . . . must try and refrain from using bad language when talking to them on the phone . . . Still, going to give them a piece of my mind though . . . Hello, St Goban's College here. The bus to take us on our school tour to France has not arrived yet . . . three hours late . . . This is disgraceful. The kids have now been waiting over three hours . . .

But, sir, excuse me. Please calm down now. Today is the 21st. You booked your school tour for the 22nd. The bus will be arriving on schedule tomorrow!

# DICK SPRING

Some years ago I was guest of honour at the People of the Year Awards. The main event, which was going out live on RTE, was a short speech by me at the end of which I announced the Person of the Year. I duly delivered my speech in a relatively competent manner (even if I say so myself). Then I announce, 'And this year's overall winner, the Person of the Year, is' — I turn over the page to find a blank page — the name was omitted! The seconds started ticking very slowly — and it felt like an eternity — I was staring at the camera. All the guests, about 600 of them, were waiting for the name. The name wasn't there!

Eventually, after a long period of silence on national TV, I remember that I have been introduced to John Parker, the CEO of Harland and Wolff, when I arrived in the Burlington Hotel some hours earlier, and he was the Person of the Year.

Luckily for me I got it and, as friends told me afterwards, I was a very relieved man — 25 seconds later — to make the announcement

# CHARLIE SWAN

I was 16 and it was my second year riding. Racing was at the Curragh and I was riding a horse called Rondout, trained by Dessie McDonagh. We were all in the stalls ready to start the one and a half mile handicap. The starter asked if everyone was ready and then let us go.

Just as we jumped from the stalls my breeches burst open. We were gone about a furlong and as I was riding so short, my breeches were around my ankles. I was trying desperately to pull them up but Christy Roche was shouting to me to leave them alone or else I would fall off and probably bring him down with me.

All the other jockeys were laughing and whistling at me, including Joanna Morgan, the only lady in the race. With the breeches still around my ankles, I came home red faced but third.

# ALICE TAYLOR

*A Warm Welcome*

When my children were young I ran a guest-house. It was on the side of the village street. People often came into the front hallway and if there was nobody about they found their way to the kitchen door and knocked. The large kitchen was a busy place.

One of my young sons found it highly amusing to knock smartly on the kitchen door and when I opened it he stood there grinning up at me and said, 'It's only me.'

He did this twice one morning and when the knock came for a third time I decided to take action. The morning paper was still on the table so I grabbed it, rolled it up firmly into a baton and made for the door. I whipped the door open and belted the paper down with venom on top of the unsuspecting head. Too late, I discovered it was a little nun collecting for charity.


# LARRY TOMPKINS

I would think the most embarrassing thing that has happened to me occurred only a few years ago.

It was 1992, the week before we played the Munster final against Kerry. Usually a week before any game I always go for a run on the Mardyke track in Cork with a friend of mine who is a runner. That particular day was warm but windy, so I jogged without any socks on. I ran for about thirty minutes and did a lot of stretching.

When we finished, we sat on the bank and watched a football game on the pitch near by. I took off my sneakers, and continued watching the game for approximately thirty minutes. When I got home, and particularly that night, my foot itched, so I took off my shoe and I saw that my instep was red and sore, but I didn't worry.

I went to training on Tuesday and I felt my foot very sore in the football boot. I informed Billy Morgan and he told me to take it easy. The next morning I went to the chemist for some cream. By Friday the skin had broken and the foot had swollen up like a balloon, so I went into the hospital and was put on antibiotics. When it came to Sunday, there was just no way I could play and Dr Con Murphy ruled me out.

The team assembled in Jury's Hotel before the game. When I arrived at Pairc Ui Chaoimh I felt very low, so I got my bag and I decided to put on my gear and see if I could get my boots on. I usually wear size 10, but with all the strapping I needed a size 11 on my right foot which I borrowed from one of the subs.

I warmed up in the gym and I was listed among the subs. During the course of the game I came on as a sub, which was a big mistake as I was very weak from the antibiotics. Everything was so embarrassing (the story was I got sunburnt). It was a nightmare.

Something that started so simply was to develop into an infection and caused a major problem. To this day people still remind me. I suppose I can laugh now, but I assure you I didn't then.

# BISHOP EAMON WALSH

*'Off the Altar'*

Playing chestnuts was in full swing, 'Conker 9' challenging 'Conker 10' for first prize of being 'Conker 20'. Even the women's sodality could not get in the way as we struck it out in the sacristy corridor while the parish priest was addressing the women. The door was slightly ajar — partially to hear what was for women's ears only, partially to know when to light the charcoal for the thurible, as well as the precautionary keeping watch.

Wham! The shoe lace of my Conker 9 slipped from my fingers, bouncing off the door on to the marble and across the sanctuary floor as far as the high altar. The contest could not be interrupted by time or preacher. Confessions had just begun and the parish priest was safely inside his confessional.

'No one would see you if the lights of the church were turned off,' advised Conker 10. 'Anyhow, people can pray better in the flickering candlelight of the shrines.'

As I crawled on my belly along the cold marble to retrieve my Conker 9, the giggles commenced behind me. I too began to tremble, quiver, giggle and eventually burst out laughing. With sweeping arms I touched the seasoned chestnut and grasped it quickly, swimming and crawling hastily back across the sanctuary. Conker 10 ran home; another went under a bench; and my best pal ducked into the press. I was stuck to the ground, speechless.

While being interrogated, I clutched Conker 9. 'You're off the altar', the parish priest bellowed. The lights were put on, exposing the fellow under the bench. 'You're off too.' The parish priest doubled back when he heard a timid voice coming from the press: 'Is he gone yet?' 'You're off the altar as well.' We were encountering a first cousin of excommunication! What would we say at home? Nothing, was the verdict that Friday night.

Saturday brought new insights. The parish priest was old and we agreed that he might forget or might not recognise us. Sunday Mass at 8 a.m. was the test. Two of us turned up. Parents knew we were listed so we risked it, foolishly.

We lined up in the middle of the procession, more angelic looking than usual. Not breathing, we prepared for the departure bell. It was round two instead as the parish priest shouted, 'I put you two off the altar. You're fired.'

Sheepishly we made our way home, passing people coming to Mass. I met my father among them — we would talk later! I had brought disgrace on everyone belonging to me.

Time is a great healer, and I'm back on the altar again!

# JIMMY WALSH

Embarrassed? I would have cheerfully swapped places with an earthward-bound parachutist whose canopy had failed to open.

The phone message from my news chief was given to me in a restaurant on the way to Hurn airport in the south of England. Put simply, it demanded: explain how the *Irish Press* is today running your story about the maiden flight of a new passenger jet, when the plane never left the ground.

For a cub reporter on his first overseas assignment, the query could not have been more embarrassing. My budding journalistic career seemed destined for a flight into oblivion.

The omens had been so promising a few days earlier, when W. J. (Bill) Redmond, stern ruler of the *Press* news desk, had called me aside. A Wexford man, with a reputation as a disciplinarian, W. J.'s credo was that facts were as sacred as life itself.

Fortunately for myself and others taken on as *Irish Press* trainees in the early 1960s, Bill had mellowed into a parental figure. But his insistence on standards remained as high as ever.

One of the three *Irish Press* executives who had interviewed me for a place on the Burgh Quay news team, he knew of my keen interest in aviation.

With a knowing twinkle in his eye, he enquired if I would like to go to England for the first proving flight of the prototype BAC 1–11. Naturally, I flew at the chance to witness a piece of flying history. The travel invitation had come from Aer Lingus which was purchasing four of the advanced rear-jet passenger aircraft.

I quickly discovered that seasoned 'hacks', Don Rooney and John Howard, would be covering the event for the *Indo* and *The Irish Times*. Their advice was to get all the background data on the plane and to write a holding story which could be published with suitable updating when the flight had taken place.

Having typed by best effort, I left instructions that it should be held back if the flight did not go ahead as scheduled, and that I would then amend it as necessary.

There was a bonus on the trip to Hurn, a visit to the British Aircraft Corporation airworks at Filton for an inspection of a full-scale mock-up of the supersonic Concorde, then at the planning stage.

But disappointment awaited. Due to bad weather, the 1–11 did not take to the air on that summer evening in 1963. The stories for the Irish national dailies would have to be put on hold, or 'rejigged' (newspaper jargon for amending). Attempts by me to get through by phone to my desk failed, but my anxiety was allayed when a member of the Aer Lingus official party assured me that a 'cancel story' message would be relayed to the *Press*. Satisfied, I joined my colleagues and our BAC hosts for dinner before retiring for the night in a plush Bournemouth hotel.

*En route* to Hurn next day, the sky fell in for this aspiring air correspondent. With no small degree of trepidation, I picked up the phone to explain what had happened. Much to my amazement, W. J. R. did not sound dire warnings about my future prospects with the *Press*. But he did ram home the message that I had breached a cardinal rule of journalism — it's the reporter's personal duty to ensure the desk is kept updated on stories.

It was a lesson I never forgot.

Neither did I ever discover how the Hurn message went astray, though there were suggestions that it had gone by mistake to the *Irish Press's* commercial offices in Dublin's O'Connell Street.

A few weeks later tragedy provided me with a chance to make amends for my 'scoop' that never was. The prototype 1–11, which had made its maiden flight a day behind schedule, crashed, killing all the technical crew on board.

I wrote a recollection piece for the *Irish Press* of that first exciting test flight.

W. J. R. expressed his approval. But my satisfaction was tempered by the knowledge that among the dead were those with whom we had celebrated and had toasted the future of the new queen of the skies.

# MARTY WHELAN

There are those in the broadcasting business who would say that every time I stand in front of a camera, it's an embarrassing moment. For them or for me? I'm never quite sure.

When you do what I do for a living, the bottom line is always to at least affect calm in front of an audience. After all, only you know that your trousers don't fit you and are being held up with the aid of three pins, or that the computer for the game show you're presenting has been acting up all day, and now here you are, live and petrified. But I digress.

Wardrobe in RTE are absolutely marvellous. They deck us all out perfectly and ensure that all our outfits are spick and span. Whatever about girl broadcasters, we boy broadcasters are sadly incapable of making sure that what we wear matches, day in, day out. So wardrobe make sure. Crisp button-down collar shirt, underpressed and clean, and trendy suit is the order of the day. But they're hardly responsible for anything.

I recall recording 'Off the Record', a chat and music series, last year, and the guest on this occasion was Terry Keane of the *Sunday Independent*. It's difficult to encounter a more elegant, more perfectly turned out woman anywhere in the world than Terry. But there we were, having the chat, cameras rolling, and it all going splendidly in a relaxed, informal way. She was a great guest and gave all that was hoped for. I'm so relaxed I decide to have a little shift in my chair, move one leg over the other, getting comfortable. Guess what I notice? The shoe I've been pointing happily at the camera for the past ten minutes has not one, but two holes in it. Then it dawned on me. Had the camera seen it? If it had, would anyone at home notice? And, more urgently, would Terry notice? To say I was temporarily mortified is the understatement of the year. I believe I got away with it on all fronts — but never again.

Wardrobe now insist on checking the soles of my shoes on every occasion. They don't trust me, and rightly so.

# Harry Whelehan

*The Pothole Wins!*

During the years I was Attorney General I became increasingly and excessively upset by the recurrence of three large potholes on the road just outside our home. When these potholes developed on previous occasions I made representations to the local authority and the necessary repairs were (after some agitation) carried out.

It would, however, have been inviting embarrassment and trouble to have made such representations while holding the office of Attorney General. Somebody, some place, would have gone to the media alleging that I was using my position to intimidate the local authority to do me a favour. A political storm would have ensued. Obviously, I wanted to avoid any such form of embarrassment.

As the years went by, the holes became deeper and wider and, in an utterly irrational way, I became wildly and disproportionately infuriated and obsessed by the existence of these potholes as they increased in depth and width.

Some months after I ceased to hold office and had returned to practise at the Bar, a friend of mine was having his drive redone. I asked him if he could arrange to save some tarmacadam for me so that I could repair the potholes myself.

My friend duly obliged and delivered a small load of the material. I immediately set to with shovel and other implements to pound the tarmacadam into my 'prize potholes' on a spring evening last year. While I was absorbed in this activity, two elderly ladies whom I did not know walked by, obviously out for an evening stroll. I said good evening to them. They looked at me, slowed their pace and continued their gaze as they passed by without returning my greeting. I should add at this stage, that I had taken care to dress appropriately for this particular job!

After they had gone five or six paces they stopped; one of them came back towards me and said: 'Excuse me. You don't mind if I ask you, but are you Mr Whelehan?' To which I replied, 'Yes, indeed I am.'

As her friend waited for her some distance down the road, she stood, put her hands on her hips, shook her head, looked straight at me and called out to her friend, her eyes still on me. 'Betty, you were right. It's him. Isn't it a shocking thing to think that a few months ago he was the Attorney General and the President of the High Court, and now the poor man is out mending the roads!'